Endorsements

In *Jesus Be the Centerfold*, Tague has masterfully diagnosed the source of the world's complacency and offered a remedy to it - authentic union with Jesus. Tague's words not only call us to a deeper faith, but they show us how to get there. Read this book and be led into an active relationship with your loving Savior.

Dave Ferguson
Exponential CEO; Author of *B.L.E.S.S.* & *Hero Maker*

Jesus Be the Centerfold challenges the superficiality of modern Christianity, urging a deeper, more committed relationship with God. With wit and vulnerability, Phill Tague invites readers on a personal and profound journey, challenging them to re-evaluate their faith and embrace a deeper, more committed relationship with God.

Bill Couchenour
Director of Deployment - Exponential

With raw honesty and compelling storytelling, Phill unpacks how many of us have unknowingly traded real, transformative faith for something far less—something comfortable, something curated, something that requires little of us but leaves us unfulfilled. This book is bold, it's convicting and it's uncomfortable in the best way possible! I pray every reader opens their heart and allows God to speak to them in ways they have never allowed Him to before. You will be grateful you did.

Heather Kittelson
Founder of Fortitude Ministries &
Ransom Church Attender

Phill Tague challenges us to move beyond a shallow, transactional faith and pursue real intimacy with God. Honest, bold, and deeply convicting, this book calls us to embrace the fullness of Christ. It's a must-read for anyone seeking a truly transformative faith!

Eric Ward
Ransom Church Attender & CEO of WS Construction

Which is the greater risk—endorsing a book about spiritual pornography or settling for a curated, caricature version of Jesus that conveniently fits within the framework of my own preferences? If you're leaning with me towards the latter, this book is absolutely calling your name and well worth the investment of your time. *Jesus be the Centerfold* is a timely, yet brutally honest wake-up call to those who have settled for shallow, airbrushed, transactional Christianity in place of real, authentic intimacy with Jesus. If you're ready to stop swiping left and settling for anything less than the fullness of Jesus, then this book is your invitation to do just that—to stop settling and say yes to Jesus for who He really is!

Torrey Martin
University Pastor, Oklahoma Wesleyan University

The title isn't clickbait. Phill Tague exposes how we settle for a superficial faith that resembles the fleeting gratification of pornography. But *Jesus be the Centerfold* is no mere bait and switch to lure you in with sexual metaphor and change subjects. Instead, he deftly weaves together the deceptive control motivating both transactional sex and transactional faith that ends in a shallow 'swipe right' distorted spirituality. The book helps us move beyond a mere 'pin-up Jesus' toward a voluntary submission to an awe-inspiring God and the intimate joy of discipleship He provides.

David Drury
Founder of more than a dozen organizations,
Author of a dozen published books including *SoulShift*.
Visit at daviddrury.com

This book is real. The choice we must all make is real. Phill leads us to seek His will and understanding (in an relatable and easy to follow manner). I would not know God without his guidance. Phill shares his faith journey and struggle in an unflinching and honest approach that helps lead us all to explore our vulnerability and our choices.

Eric Schofield
Ransom Attender & CFO/partner at WS Construction

Don't let the title fool you. This book isn't merely about sex or centerfolds. With the heart of a pastor and the gift of a storyteller, Phill Tague calls us to rethink the many ways we choose lifeless images of the good life over life-giving intimacy with God and others. It's a risky and rewarding read, not least because it points us to the REAL Jesus over cheap alternatives.

Joshua M. McNall
Oklahoma Wesleyan University,
Author of *Long Story Short* and *How Jesus Saves*

PROFOUND BOOK! Phill takes the hidden, unspeakable, and mundane parts of our lives - puts unspoken words to feelings and experiences - courageously speaks from his own vulnerability - wraps it into biblical and theological understanding with great HOPE personally, and for the church and community. This is not a quick read. It is a book that is transformational for generations.

Jo Anne Lyon
General Superintendent Emerita,
The Wesleyan Church

Pastor Tague offers a forthright and compelling argument that as Christians we have settled for far less than the real thing - the fullness in Christ that we are called to live, the beautiful relationship God wants with us. We have settled, suggests Tague, for "spiritual pornography" - a substitute that is far less than the real thing. Written in a conversational manner based on his real-life relationship experiences, he offers a comparison to what we are really called for and who we are called to be and what it takes. Tague walks us through the impact of contemporary culture's distorted view of relationship and love on our relationship with the Lord and offers practical and persuasive questions and suggestions on how to embrace the "real thing," the true loving relationship offered to each of us by our Heavenly Father.

Colleen R. Derr
EdD President and CAO, Eastern Nazarene College

Phill is an honest, natural storyteller who invites readers on a transformative spiritual journey. In his book, he challenges us not to compromise but surrender fully to all that Jesus has for us. You will be inspired to resist settling for anything less than ALL of Jesus. It's a must-read for anyone seeking a profound spiritual awakening or reawakening!

Patrick O'Connell
Global Director, NewThing

When I first read the title: *Jesus be the Centerfold: Choosing Covenant Faith Over Airbrushed Christianity*, I paused to think of why I might not want to endorse this book. Then I read it. It's raw. It's real. If you are interested in what it takes to crave an ongoing, authentic, relationship with Jesus Christ instead of settling for the phony depictions of what it means to follow Jesus that so many have imagined in their minds, you will be interested in what Phill Tague has penned with graphic orthodoxy. Stop treating the God of the Bible like a transaction to get what you want. Seek a genuine, loving, meaningful relationship with the only God of all time who calls you His beloved and offers you the invitation to love Him back with all your heart, soul, mind, and strength.

Dr. Jim Dunn
President, Oklahoma Wesleyan University

Phill has been leading a life-giving church for many years. And now he's bringing his courage and candor with an honest look at the church in America—a church that is looking less and less like Jesus. It's a twist on the title to arrest what's at risk for all of us. You have a lot of books to choose from, put this one on your 'must read' list.

Kevin Myers
Founding Pastor, 12Stone Church

I've known Phill as a pastor, but more importantly as a friend, for years. This book is an open letter to the Church straight from Phill's heart. Is it challenging? Yes. Is it brutally honest? For sure. Is this exactly what the Church needs to hear about striving for an all-encompassing faith in Jesus rather than settling for the comfort we're all too used to? Absolutely! Everyone who calls themselves a Christian needs to read this book and prepare to be shaken up (in the best way). I know I was! I'm endlessly thankful for Phill's words here, and his continued encouragement in my life.

Adam Weber
Lead Pastor of Embrace Church,
Author, host of *The Conversation* podcast

With engaging creative writing, authentic personal vulnerability, and deep biblical insight, Pastor Phill Tague writes a life-changing book. The truths he illuminates are lasers that sever chains and offer the intimacy and freedom we all crave. I am now "chasing the success of obedience" thanks to the Spirit working through Pastor Phill's words. Don't just read it, buy it for someone you love.

Larry Walkemyer, D.Min
FREE METHODIST CHURCH USA,
Strategic Catalyst for Multiplication
EXPONENTIAL,
Director of Equipping & Spiritual Engagement,
LIGHT & LIFE, Global Pastor
AZUSA PACIFIC UNIVERSITY, Trustee

Jesus, be the Centerfold

Jesus, be the Centerfold

Choosing Covenant Faith over Airbrushed Christianity

Phill Tague

Printed in the United States of America.

Throne Publishing Group
Sioux Falls, SD 57108
ThronePG.com

Table of Contents

To my wife, Stephani.
Your love for me even in moments
where I haven't loved you well has taught me
in real time just how powerful covenants are.

Foreword

Hey friend.

As a pastor in the same mid-sized (but growing!) city as Phill, I've known him for what feels like forever. But for years, that's all Phill was to me: a great pastor at one of the other growing churches in town.

That all changed when, years back, I went through a really hard season in my church. It was the lowest year of my life. That time made me question who I was, what I was called to, and if I should just give up and walk away from the Church entirely. If I'm honest, I even questioned whether or not I wanted to keep following Jesus.

In the middle of those months filled with anxiety, embarrassment, and discouragement, Phill frequently reached out to see how I was doing. Texting me. Grabbing coffee. Going on double dates with our wives. Phill was a gift from God. And through that time, Phill showed me a glimpse of the real Jesus, not some empty airbrushed version of him. Several years later, I was able to reach out and do the same for Phill when he went through a harder season himself.

The gift from those hard times? In the midst of all that criticism, doubt, and questioning was this: we were no longer just two pastors who shared a zip code—we were friends.

Which is why I'm so excited that you've picked up this book. Because my friend Phill wrote it.

This is a book that many don't know they're searching for. Why? Because it shares about a version of Jesus that they don't know they're missing.

Daily it seems like there's a new writeup or stat that comes out about the number of people walking away from Jesus and the Church. But the truth is, these individuals aren't walking away from Jesus (at least not the Jesus Phill knows), they're walking away from the cheap, airbrushed version of Christianity they've been told to believe is the real deal.

As humans, including myself, we routinely settle for the cheap version of things.

Cheap thrills.

Instant gratification.

A dopamine hit that will keep us going only long enough until the next one.

But I don't want the fake, watered-down version of Jesus.

I want the real Jesus.

Even if that Jesus asks us to surrender everything.

I want the real Jesus who won't put up with our excuses and our crap.

I want the real Jesus who makes us more like himself everyday.

This Jesus—this covenant faith—might cost us our lives and all that we are. Yet, he's worth it.

On every page Phill's words are refreshingly honest—honest about himself and the struggles he's gone through, and even more so, honest about all that Jesus is to him. Phill chooses to share a not-so-pretty struggle in his personal life—the battle against pornography—as a metaphor for how we've bent and distorted Jesus into a vehicle for our personal satisfaction. It might be shocking to hear it put that way, but it's true.

We're all hungry for the real version of Jesus, for him to be at the center of our lives and hearts and transform us in the way only he can. Phill is going to walk us through how to meet that Jesus and ditch the one we've been clinging to for so long. I, for one, can't wait to be along for that ride.

Phill's friend,
Adam

Adam Weber
Lead Pastor of Embrace Church,
Author, podcast host, Cincinnati Bengals fan

INTRODUCTION

Jesus be the Centerfold

How we've settled for so much less than all of Jesus.

I remember exactly where I was when it happened. That moment is forever emblazoned in my mind. When I rode my bike to my friend's house that day, I had no idea it was going to happen. I think if I would have known, I would have pedaled as fast as my nine-year-old legs could carry me away from that place … and from that choice.

I only lived a few houses away. For the rest of my childhood and into middle school and then high school, the temptation would loom so large just a few blocks away.

Over the coming years, I would at times try to avoid going over to his house. At other times, I would find excuses to be there. And any time I was there, it was like there was a magnetic pull to that box. In that room. In that closet.

The decisions I made in the dark in my childhood still haunt me. It's not the shame—I've long since let go of that. I serve a God who loves me so unconditionally. What haunts me is what it cost me to settle. I settled in those moments for so much less than God's plan for me. And I settled not just once but over and over again. For a while, I had resigned myself to this reality. What haunts me is the cost of settling for less than all God had for me.

You see, it was in that house just down the street, where I had played so many afternoons with my best friend, that I was first exposed to pornography. Up until that day, that house was home away from home. It was safe. It was filled with incredible memories of Excite Bike, Mike Tyson's Punch Out, backyard home run derbies, and more "Weird Al" Yankovic than anyone should justify listening to. That was my memory of that sacred space in my life. Until that day.

In truth, my friend was sharing with me, and not with anyone else. I was the person he trusted with his discovery.

His sharing with me was instinctual, as we shared everything with each other. He had made a discovery that, to any nine-year-old male, was filled with both disgust and an insatiable curiosity. I remember that day that his parents were gone. I remember walking into his parents' room, which we were never allowed to do when they were there. (As a parent, I now totally understand this rule!)

I remember the smell of the room—a mix of aftershave and some sort of flowery perfume, both of which made me feel like his parents were lurking right around the corner. I remember the sound of the squeaky accordion closet door as it struggled against its hinges, almost begging me to stop. I remember when the light hit the box, and for the first time, I could see its contents. It was a big box. A stack. And on the top of the stack of magazines was what I believe was Miss August 1987. The title across the top of the page? PLAYBOY.

Now, let me pause this story for a moment to make a clarification. This is not a book about pornography. It's not a woeful tale of struggle punctuated at the end with a perfect recipe for overcoming said struggle. This is a book about settling. Pornography is the metaphor, and one that fits all too well what most Christians are guilty of ... settling. Too often, we settle for a picture of Jesus we like. One that works for us. But it's not real. It's airbrushed. So back to our story.

I remember so many details of that day that I wish I could forget. Mostly, I remember the feeling. More accurately, the mix of feelings. Much later in my life, as I wrestled with a pornography addiction that started before I had even learned about the birds and the bees, I remember thinking, "This must be what Adam and Eve felt like when they made their terrible choice." And every time I gave in to that temptation, I felt the same feelings I had felt that very first time. It was easy to relate to Adam and Eve. I knew what I was. I knew what I'd done. Mostly, I knew this wasn't God's will for me.

In the Bible, in the book of Genesis, we read about that encounter for Adam and Eve. As the serpent whispered lies to Eve, you can literally feel her emotions coming off the pages of scripture. God had been very clear what His plan was for them. He had given them everything. He walked with them in the garden. He gave them one rule: Do not eat from the tree in the center of the garden. If you do, you will surely die.

> 4 *"You won't die!" the serpent replied to the woman.*
> 5 *"God knows that your eyes will be opened as soon as you eat it, and you will be like God, knowing both good and evil."*
> 6 *The woman was convinced. She saw that the tree was beautiful and its fruit looked delicious, and she wanted the*

> *wisdom it would give her. So she took some of the fruit and ate it. Then she gave some to her husband, who was with her, and he ate it, too.* (Genesis 3:4–6 NLT)

I resonate with all those feelings. What I saw was beautiful. The fruit looked delicious. I wanted the wisdom it would give me (I wanted to know what was inside). I was convinced. That day in 1987, I was convinced. Over the next decade or more, the serpent would continue to whisper, "You won't die." And every time, I felt these things. And every time, I was convinced.

What I felt wasn't just lust. It was control.

When I gave in that day and every time after that, what I was seeking in that moment was not just the satiation of lust. I was feeding my need for control. And not just control in general but a very specific kind of control. I'll unpack that more in a moment, but first, I need to tell you about the second thing I felt. Again, I learned so much about myself from Adam and Eve's account with the serpent.

> 7 *At that moment their eyes were opened, and they suddenly felt shame at their nakedness. So they sewed fig leaves together to cover themselves.* (Genesis 3:7 NLT)

I felt exposed. Completely and utterly exposed.

Scripture describes this as "shame at their nakedness." But nakedness wasn't even something they fully understood.

They had been created naked, but with no shame. What was new wasn't the nakedness. It was the shame. It was the reality of exposure.

It may be from that day forward, humanity has been hiding.

And that's what I did. For years, I hid. I hid, and I grabbed for control. I grabbed for a feeling, and I grabbed for it on my terms.

A year or so later, the box was gone.

It wouldn't be until many years later, as I wrestled with my own struggle with pornography, that I would look back to the very first divorce I remember ever being aware of and wonder if that box had played a part in it.

He chose the box over his wife. He left his kids. He took the box. I would argue it wasn't even about the magazines. It was about control. He chose magazines over relationships.

He chose images over intimacy. He chose control.

So back to our metaphor. I will double down—this book isn't about pornography. But this is our metaphor. And I think it's the perfect metaphor to have a conversation about the church.

I've been a pastor for a long time now. Long enough to watch generations of Christians struggle in a thousand different ways with the exact same thing. And every time I see it, I think of my story. I think of that box. And I think of the choices we all make.

There is a phrase I have used to describe this settling in our local church context—It's like we're creating spiritual pornography.

Spiritual pornography is a picture of choices. It's about choosing control over surrender. It's about choosing a caricature over the real thing. It's about choosing a picture in our head over a relationship in our hearts. It's about choosing images over intimacy. That's what this book it about.

I'm writing this book to all the Christians who have settled. I'm writing to Christians who have not found what they are looking for in their faith, never realizing they are actually looking in the wrong place. I'm writing to Christians who know something is missing in their faith.

This journey won't be easy. It will be raw. But it will also be real. And that will actually be the hardest part. Real is what it is. You can take it or leave it, but you can't change it. Real includes lots of things we love but also lots of things we don't. You can't whitewash real. You can't make it fit your life. You actually have to fit your life to it. Real is costly. And that's why most people avoid or ignore it and settle for less.

But here's the best part.

It's REAL.

What God has for you is real. What Jesus did for you is real.

The relationship and the covenant Jesus calls us into is real.

If you are sick of settling, there is more. Don't settle. Keep reading. After that, the choice is yours.

Ready? Let's go.

CHAPTER 1

Cheap Thrill

Choosing comfort over commitment and why we always settle for less.

I didn't tell you this about myself in the introduction, but I'm kind of a big deal.

Not movie-star big or sports-icon big. Certainly nothing like that. But in the realm of biblical knowledge among eight to fourteen year olds, I was basically royalty. It was during that season of my life that I was part of an elite group of young, up-and-coming Pharisees known as Junior Bible Quizzers.

And not only was I a Bible quizzer (and a good one, I might add), I was what's known in certain very small circles of the world as a "master quizzer." What's a master quizzer, you might ask? It's right there in the name. I was one of the few individuals on the Junior Bible Quiz circuit who had mastered every question in the quiz box. All 365. Memorized. Owned. Nailed it.

Now, there was no real prize other than a general recognition of the accomplishment (although my dad DID have a trophy designed for me with a special place to hold the box with all the cards). But I have to admit—when I walked into every Bible quiz match, I could hear the whispers and feel the stares. *It's him. It's the master quizzer.* I'd be lying if I said it didn't feel pretty good.

Now, if you're paying attention, you may have noticed this was all going down at the same time I was developing my addiction to my friend's dad's *Playboy* collection. I was simultaneously being sucked into a private nightmare of my own making AND memorizing 365 questions and scripture verses about the Old and New Testaments. One for each day of the year.

For those of you reading this who claim to be Christ followers, I wonder if you have found yourself in a similar place in life. I wonder if you've ever walked that tightrope of public perception and private prison. I wonder if you've ever been able to relate to the Apostle Paul, as he laments an internal battle in all of us who seem on our own strength to live out this thing called the Christian faith. Paul writes in Romans chapter 7:

> [14] *So the trouble is not with the law, for it is spiritual and good. The trouble is with me, for I am all too human, a slave to sin.* [15] *I don't really understand myself, for I want to do what is right, but I don't do it. Instead, I do what I hate.* [16] *But if I know that what I am doing is wrong, this shows that I agree that the law is good.* [17] *So I am not the one doing wrong; it is sin living in me that does it.* (Romans 7:14-17 NLT)

I can totally relate to that phrase—I am all too human. One of my dear friends, Pastor Phil Wiseman, founding Pastor of Table Church in Des Moines, Iowa, made this statement about our humanity:

> *It's actually inaccurate to sin and then blame our humanity. We say things like 'I'm only human!' when we mess up, as though that is what we were made to do. In reality, we were*

made in the image of God, so we are most human when we are seeking His image in our lives. After all, Jesus never sinned, and he was fully human—you might even say more human than us, because his humanity wasn't tainted by sin. A more appropriate response when we sin would be 'forgive my inhumanity...that was so unlike Jesus.'

Forgive my inhumanity. I can't tell you how many times I could accurately utter those words. I grew up in a Christian home. I was a master quizzer. I was a kid who knew the word of God and who wanted in my heart to obey it. And most of the time, I did.

Except when I didn't.

Now, if you're a proclaimed Christ follower and you say you can't relate, you're lying to someone. It might be me, or it might just be yourself, but someone isn't getting the full truth.

The full truth is that this struggle is as old as humanity. From the creation of humans in God's image, we have struggled to live up to our design. God made us for a deep and intimate relationship with Him. He created us in His image. He created us, male and female, to be reflections of Him. He created us with the capacity for choice, and He offered us Himself.

You were created for intimacy with God.

But to say humanity struggles with intimacy issues would be beyond an understatement. I think the struggles we see around human intimacy are nothing more than a flesh-riddled reflection of our greater spiritual intimacy issues. From Adam and Eve in the garden, to the Israelites in the wilderness, to the Pharisees and religious leaders who made God seem out of reach and who rejected Jesus at every turn, **humanity has an almost perfect track record of settling for less.**

I think in our current cultural context, we struggle in general with the idea of intimacy with God. In no way is this limited to one group of people or one gender. But I can only speak from my perspective. I can only see the world through my eyes.

I'm a dude. In the twenty-first century. In the United States. I remember as a kid hearing about this idea of an intimate personal relationship with God and feeling almost weird about it. I knew it was something I was supposed to want. I knew it was a good thing, or at least that's what I was told. But just the phrase—intimacy with God—seemed weird to me.

Part of this discomfort is, I believe, because we live in a hyper-sexualized culture, where intimacy is almost always connected in our minds to sex. I've been married twenty-two years (at the time of this writing), and I can attest from personal experience—sex is good. I approve. Ten out of ten.

But what I have found in over twenty years of marriage is that while sex is good, intimacy is better. And sex as an expression of intimacy within a biblical marriage is unparalleled. You can have sex and not be intimate. In fact, most of the sexuality we see in our world isn't an expression of intimacy. It's just flesh. It's physical, not emotional.

But intimacy with my wife is different. Intimacy with God seemed weird to me as a kid because in my young reptile brain, intimacy = sex = being naked. But after many years of marriage, what I have learned is that while sex CAN be an expression of intimacy, the real truth is much deeper.

The reason nakedness CAN feel intimate is because nothing is hidden. Nakedness is not the same as intimacy, but true intimacy always involves some level of exposure. The reason being naked with my wife is intimate is because in that vulnerable state, I am fully known by my wife and still loved. And THAT is the nature of intimacy.

Intimacy is being fully known and still fully loved.

I love how one of my friends, author Chase Rashad, put it in his book *Seamless*:

> *The first humans were completely vulnerable before Creator and one another. With every lump, bump and foll exposed to high heaven, they didn't think twice about it.*

Wow. How beautiful is that. How powerful. Chase goes on to express how "Shame is the diminishing of one's sense of identity and social standing." He describes Adam and Eve as "physically, emotionally, psychologically, and spiritually vulnerable before God and each other, and they were completely content with it."

That is intimacy. It's God's will for us—with Him and with those nearest to us. Certainly it's His plan for marriage. And I have, year over year, found more of this with my wife. And that has only grown over time. The older I get, the more intimate our relationship becomes. As we age, and as life takes a toll on our physical bodies, what we bring to the table is a self that is scarred by life, weathered by time, and yet carries the marks of a life lived together. And the intimacy we share comes from being fully known—physically, mentally, emotionally, spiritually—and still chosen. That is intimacy. It's so costly. It's so scary. It's so much harder than anyone can tell you. And it's so worth it.

This is what God is offering. It's what He longs for with you. It's what you were created for. The God of the Universe, who created life, who knew you while you were still in your mother's womb, wants an intimate relationship with you. He wants you to know that you are fully known and yet still fully loved. So many Christians hide their lives behind a facade, hoping no one sees what's beneath the surface. I know. I did it for decades. And yet nothing is actually hidden from God. He sees you. He knows you intimately. But intimacy isn't one way. God is waiting for us to choose Him.

I remember my first girlfriend. I remember my first kiss. I remember the first mixtape I ever made for a girl—heavy on Chicago and Air Supply (if you know, you know). From the time I realized girls didn't actually have cooties, I have leaned into love.

My wife would probably call me a romantic at heart. I think she's right. I love love. I love what love feels like. I had a lot of girlfriends growing up, not because I needed a relationship or anything like that but because I love love.

Unfortunately, that means I also know a lot about heartbreak. I know what it feels like to put yourself out there and to not have the love returned. I know what it feels like to be broken up with. I know what it's like to give too much of yourself away to someone who isn't trustworthy with your heart. I've heard those dreaded words, "I don't love you anymore."

I think love carries an inherent sense of risk. Far too many people know what it feels like being on the wrong side of intimacy gone wrong. As a result, I think a lot of our world today has determined the risks associated with love aren't worth it. We put up walls. We protect our hearts. We still date. We still pursue relationships. We just do so at a surface level. We aren't looking for intimacy. We're just looking for a cheap thrill. A quick fix. No strings attached.

We're looking for intimacy but without the risk.

And while in some cases, we do avoid the risk, we also avoid intimacy because intimacy is an inherently risky endeavor. I think this mindset has invaded the church and has infiltrated our search for faith. As I look around at the church, specifically the church in the United States, what I see most of the time is cheap faith. I see people settling for just enough. Just enough of Jesus. Just enough of church. Just enough religion. For so many, church is defined by the question, "What's the minimum requirement for salvation?"

Imagine asking yourself that question in marriage. "What's the least I need to do to qualify as still married?" Imagine how you would feel as a spouse if the person you married said to you, "Look, I'm not looking for intimacy in this marriage. Sure, I'll take any benefit this marriage will offer me, but I'm not really interested in going deep. I want joint filing status, every once in a while I'd like you to meet my needs, but beyond that, I'm not really interested in more."

You might say, "Listen, I'm not getting married to God." You're right. What God is asking for is far more intimate than marriage.

> [25] *A large crowd was following Jesus. He turned around and said to them,* [26] *"If you want to be my disciple, you must, by comparison, hate everyone else—your father and mother, wife and children, brothers and sisters—yes, even your own life. Otherwise, you cannot be my disciple.* [27] *And if you do not carry your own cross and follow me, you cannot be my disciple.* (Luke 14:25-27 NLT)

This passage tends to hit the ears of modern-day listeners in a way that leaves them at the very least uncomfortable, if not actually offended. How could Jesus want me to hate my family? How could He expect me to devalue those I love? Let me put you at ease—He doesn't.

This isn't a statement at all about how much you love your family. This is a statement about how much **more** Jesus expects that we are to love Him. This is Jesus' call to a deeper level of relationship than you have with anyone else on this planet. This is Jesus calling you into intimacy. How else could He ever expect you to carry your own cross and follow Him? You aren't going to live in a way that requires self-denial unless it's for someone you love more than you love yourself. Someone you love more than anything. Someone actually worth dying for.

As I observe the church in the United States, I do not see most people living with this level of self-denial in their faith. Yes, they want Jesus as a part of their lives. Yes, they value what church adds to their life. But I would be hard-pressed to describe their relationship with God as "intimate." I watch as we all prioritize our family and our own lives over our faith. I see this in myself all the time. It's hard to count the cost, to deny myself and to take up my cross. It's easy to choose comfort over commitment. Comfort is ... well ... comfortable. Commitment—not so much.

If there's one thing the enemy loves, it's when he can get us to settle for less than all of Jesus. Less than all God has for us. Less than intimacy.

In Genesis 3, when we read the account of Adam and Eve in the garden as they are being tempted by the serpent, he tempted Adam and Eve with something very specific. God had laid out a very specific plan for this intimate relationship with Adam and Eve. When the serpent begins to whisper, he is questioning God's plan.

> [4] *"You won't die!" the serpent replied to the woman.* [5] *"God knows that your eyes will be opened as soon as you eat it, and you will be like God, knowing both good and evil."* [6] *The woman was convinced. She saw that the tree was beautiful and its fruit looked delicious, and she wanted the wisdom it would give her. So she took some of the fruit and ate it. Then she gave some to her husband, who was with her, and he ate it, too.* (Genesis 3:4–6 NLT)

You won't die.

He goes on to tempt Adam and Eve with three common temptations. She saw the tree was beautiful (lust of the eyes). She saw the fruit looked delicious (lust of the flesh). She wanted the wisdom it would give her (pride of life). These three temptations are at the core of our intimacy issues. They perpetually keep us asking the question, "What if there's something better out there?" They perpetually keep us from committing, from settling in, from surrendering. What the enemy was promising Adam and Eve was the ability to obtain God's promise without counting the cost.

Fast-forward to the temptation of Jesus in the New Testament. The Spirit led Jesus into the wilderness to be tempted by the enemy. As He is fasting for forty days, Jesus faces three temptations in Luke chapter 4:

"Tell these stones to become bread." (lust of the flesh)
"I'll give you the world if you bow to me." (lust of the eyes)
"Prove you're God—jump off the temple." (pride of life)

Satan was offering Jesus the ability to obtain God's promise without counting the cost. Look at the middle promise in particular. "I'll give you the world if you bow to me." Jesus was there to save the world. That's why He had come. Satan offers Jesus the same thing God was offering but without any of the sacrifice.

You can have the world without the cross.

And isn't that what Satan is always tempting us with? The call of the Christian faith is a call to intimacy. It's a call to deny yourself, take up your cross, and follow Him. And the lie the enemy continues to whisper into our ears is just the same as the lie he whispered to Eve in the garden. You can have the world without the cross.

If you're a proclaimed Christian and you're reading this, I want to challenge you to take stock of your relationship with God right now. The goal of this book is in no way to get Christians to question their faith. For those who have true faith and who are living in a truly intimate relationship with God, nothing you've read so far has you questioning anything. You are secure in your very real, very costly, very intimate relationship with your heavenly Father. That intimacy comes from being fully known—physically, mentally, emotionally, spiritually—and still chosen. Your faith is so costly. It's so scary. It's so much harder than anyone could have ever told you. And it's so worth it.

But if you have reached this point of the book, and you don't feel the security that is only found in a deep and intimate love relationship with your Savior, you may feel that deep sense of questioning. Take it from this Junior Bible Quizzer ... there's more.

I remember when I discovered a real, true, intimate relationship with my wife. Every day, I count the cost of that relationship. Every day, I choose it. When I found the real thing, one of the things that struck me most is how convinced I had been in other relationships that what I had was real. But those relationships weren't that much different than the relationship I had early in my life with pornography. They were full of me looking for all the benefits of intimacy without any of the costs. But with intimacy, there is always a cost.

If that's what you're feeling right now, your faith may be masquerading as more than it is. If your faith is defined by looking for all the benefits of intimacy with God without any of the costs of that relationship ... if as you live out your faith, you can't see your cross, you may have settled for the "cheap thrill" of cultural Christianity, and you may have traded true intimacy for spiritual pornography.

CHAPTER 2

Pin-up Jesus

Who Jesus is vs. who we make Him to be.

What does God look like? This is not a new question. A simple Google search will reward you with lots of different caricatures of God—pictures we have created in our minds based on a whole host of different perceptions of the divine.

You've got the classic old man with the long white beard. You've got those who see God like an angry teacher with a ruler, ready to rap you on the back of the hand at the first infraction. One of my favorite caricatures of God is actually Morgan Freeman's portrayal of God in the movie Evan Almighty. I personally love the idea of a God who rejoices in who we are, who joins us in a celebration dance, and who laughs with joy just because He loves spending time with us.

But you notice the dangerous phrase I used there? It's a

phrase that has gotten a lot of us in trouble when it comes to our understanding of God.

I personally love...

If you read the Bible, there will be things about God that you personally love. There will also be some things you don't love so much. There will be things you agree with and things you have a hard time reconciling.

Fortunately for you and me, we live in a postmodern culture, where truth is relative and you are able to choose or create whatever version of truth works best for you. How convenient. (I hope you note my sarcasm here because I'm laying it on pretty thick.)

In the first century, Jewish culture was anything but postmodern. Truth was truth. And God's law was at the center of the Jewish understanding of truth. The temple was the center of society, and everything revolved around the Law. God had given Israel the Ten Commandments, and their entire society was based around these ten unchanging truth statements from God.

And yet as time passed, the religious leaders who were in charge of upholding the law began to interpret the law and to make new laws based off of those interpretations. Over time, these additional laws began to paint a picture in the religious leaders' minds of what God was like.

Meanwhile, the people of God were growing further and further from Him. They were mixing in the ideologies of the world they lived in with their Jewish culture, justifying more and more outside influence and blending the worship of other gods with their worship of the one true God. Eventually, they became so rebellious that God allowed them to be taken into exile. Over time, living in exile shaped their view of who their coming Messiah would be. Prophets for centuries had shared prophecies about a coming Messiah—a Savior. The religious leaders had painted one picture of that Messiah in their heads. The people of Israel had painted a completely different picture. But both groups were guilty of doing the same thing:

They were painting a picture of the Savior they wanted.

• • •

I remember the first time I got caught looking at pornography. The box had become a big part of my life at this point. Every time I gave in to the box, the shame burned a little dimmer and the temptation burned a little hotter. At first, my friend and I only ventured a peek in the box when we were left alone in the house. It was too risky any other time to sneak into his parents' room.

Eventually, though, for reasons I can't fully explain, the box relocated. I remember because my friend and I were left alone one day, and almost immediately, we were drawn like moths to a flame toward the secret hiding spot of the box. The door squeaked open as usual, light flooded the closet floor as usual. But there, where the box used to sit, there was nothing but a small square indentation in the carpet—the fading proof of the box's presence. I remember being incredibly disappointed. I also remember being incredibly relieved. There was still a part of my soul that was very much alive that knew what we were doing was not okay and was not pleasing to God. Perhaps this was His gift to me. Perhaps He was making a way out.

A week later, my friend called me. He had found the box.

He said he hadn't been looking for it. He said he stumbled upon it. That may be true. But if there's one thing I know about pre-teen boys and sexual temptation, it's that the pull is strong. Either way, the box was back. And this time, it was an even worse temptation for us because of its location.

The box was in the basement. Alone. Far from supervision. The basement that was filled with toys. The basement where my friend's mom would often send us to play for hours. The windowless, hidden from the world, away from the prying eyes of any parental authority figures, basement.

Before I knew it, the box became a regular part of our routine. It didn't matter if parents were there. In the hidden confines of the basement, it was just us and the box. Eventually, the box became our reason for hanging out. No pretense of playing anymore. Just the box. We used to take turns in the closet with the box while the other one watched and listened for any unwanted intruders into our secret domain.

It was that safety within our secret space, secure in the lies we were telling ourselves, that eventually we let our guard down. I didn't even hear his mom coming. There was no hiding what we were doing. Both of us had magazines in front of us. Both of us were enthralled in what we were seeing. Both of us were staring at the centerfold.

For those who have been blessed in being fully protected from this world, the centerfold is a larger than life, fold-out image of a woman in all her glory. I must admit, though, it felt anything but glorious feeling his mom's presence over my shoulder.

I don't remember my dad ever being angrier with me than he was when he got that phone call. I remember being grounded from that house for a LONG time. But what I remember more than my father's anger was his disappointment. He told me I should be ashamed of myself. Don't worry, Dad. I've got shame covered.

In reality, shame didn't begin to describe what I was feeling in that moment. I didn't know enough about God at the time to know that conviction and shame are very different. Conviction is a tool God uses to remind us of His will and to try to call us back on the right path. Conviction is what I had been feeling for months. Conviction was what I had been ignoring.

But shame—that's a tool of the enemy. Conviction addresses what we have done—you have done something bad. Shame is the enemy, telling us who we are—you ARE bad. That's what I felt in those moments. I felt like I was bad. Broken. Unredeemable. I felt ashamed.

After the initial anger had burned away, my dad tried to talk to me about the dangers of pornography. He was well-meaning. He was trying to help. But his approach didn't pack the punch I think he was hoping it would in my prepubescent mind.

"Son, those pin-ups aren't even real. They are just airbrushed images made to look perfect."

My father was trying to appeal to me rationally about the danger of setting up a false image of something in my head. But I was ten at the time—I hadn't quite reached rational yet. I didn't care that those images weren't real. I cared about the control I felt when I looked at them. I cared about how they made me feel. And I was way too willing to settle for a pin-up version of sexuality. Despite my dad's best efforts to dissuade me, and despite my knowledge this wasn't real, and despite knowing it was hurting me ... I kept going back to the box.

I share this story of my life with you to illustrate a truth, one that has had a significant impact on our lives and on what we believe.

We are living our lives in an airbrushed reality.

Despite knowing what we believe isn't real, and despite knowing what we are choosing may actually be hurting us, most of us still choose to settle for so much less. In a world where truth is seen as relative, we can actually make our lives whatever we want them to be. We can use social media to present an airbrushed picture of our entire lives. We post only the pictures we want people to see. We share only the stories that paint us in a certain light. We curate the content of our lives to the point where many people actually believe their curated life is their real life—the life they deserve at any cost.

For most people, this has led them to a life void of any sort of faith. But for those who claim to have a relationship with Jesus, this propensity to whitewash our lives and to curate our reality has had a profound impact on how we tend to live out our faith. Any time you are curating the content of your life, there comes a point where reality doesn't work for you. Reality is too messy to fit into the confines of our curated lives. There simply isn't room for all of Jesus. My faith in Jesus plays well up to a point, but eventually, Jesus starts crossing some lines, setting some boundaries, declaring things as "wrong" and even "sinful"—things that the world around us celebrates.

And so a lot of Christians make a choice. I actually don't think they realize they are making it even as it's happening. It's so subtle, it almost doesn't feel like a conscious choice. Slowly, over time, most Christians choose to recreate Jesus into an image that works for them. We "fit" Jesus into our lives. Slowly but surely, we create Jesus in our image. We airbrush our picture of Jesus until what's in front of us isn't even real anymore. It's a pin-up version of Jesus.

If we would actually read God's word in the Bible, we would see things that conflict with the choices we're making—but that's not a problem, as most Christians don't actually read or know God's word. If we knew God's word, it would actually deal a death blow to this pin-up version of our Savior. In His word, our heavenly Father is trying to appeal to us rationally about the danger of setting up a false image of something in our heads. But most Christians aren't rational. We don't care if the images in our mind aren't real. We care about having control of this whole faith thing. We care about how Jesus makes us feel. We care about what people think of us, and we care about the curated content of our lives. And this makes us way too willing to settle for a pin-up version of Jesus.

The first century was social media-free but far from drama-free. And in a way, the Jewish people were just as interested in curating the content of their lives as we are today. Religious leaders in particular were interested in the control that came from being the curators of religious life. They created rules and regulations they claimed were designed to keep us from wandering from God, but ultimately these rules and laws gave religious leaders almost total societal control. These leaders knew the prophecies about a Messiah, a deliverer, but they had their own version of this Messiah in their minds—and, no surprise, he was a perfect representation of their interpretation of the law—one who would keep the law perfectly.

Meanwhile, the average Jew was just trying to make it through the day. They were being oppressed by religious elite. They were living in captivity in Rome. Everything in their lives felt unsustainable. When they read the prophecies about the Messiah, they were painting a much different picture. To them, the greatest deliverance they needed in their lives was a deliverance from every form of oppression. The Messiah became, in their minds, a mighty hero, a military conqueror—a deliverer who would enter the scene and physically deliver them from their current daily realities.

Is it any wonder they missed Jesus? Born in an obscure town outside of Jerusalem to a teenage girl and her fiancé. Born in a barn or cave and laid in an animal feeding trough. Everything about His birth, while obscure and unexpected, actually fulfilled prophecies about the Messiah. But it's hard to see clearly when you already have a picture in your head. It's hard to see the Messiah born into squalor right in front of you when you have an airbrushed picture of who the Messiah would be in your head.

The Messiah was born. Prophecies were fulfilled. The world missed it.

When Jesus began His public ministry, it was full of healing and deliverance and miracles. It was full of proclamations by Jesus and by others that He was the Messiah, the son of God. He claimed to be God, and then He backed it up. But it was an uphill climb for so many Jews, not because of a lack of evidence of who He was but because He did not fit with the picture they had in their heads.

Pharisees and religious leaders were looking for a Jesus that would follow all of their rules. Nope. Jesus didn't do that.

The Jewish people were looking for political deliverance from Rome. They wanted a mighty conqueror on a noble steed, not a rabbi entering Jerusalem on a baby donkey.

Jesus wasn't the Messiah they thought they were looking for, and so they had no choice but to reject Him.

In our current context, we don't have to reject Jesus outright—we can just reshape Him into an image that works for our lives. We can airbrush our idea of Jesus. We can get Him to fit comfortably within the image we have in our heads—the picture of who we want Him to be. We can form Him any way we want, bending Jesus to fit our desires. And perhaps the scariest part of this is that no one will call us on it. And even if they do, society has trained us to reject any opinions that don't align with the one we want to hold.

No one will hold you accountable to the truth. You can choose your own truth. What the world **will** hold you accountable for is tolerance. Love has been redefined in our culture. Love means accepting me as I am, tolerating all my choices and beliefs, honoring my truth. But what no one has tolerance for is to be told they are wrong. Or even that there is such a thing as right and wrong. To tell me something I am doing is wrong is intolerant. It's hateful. How dare you?

And in the end, that leaves those of us who claim to believe in Jesus with a choice. Either we will choose to follow Jesus as He is and as God's word presents Him, or we will follow centerfold Jesus. A pin-up. An airbrushed image of the son of God that isn't even real, but boy, it's pretty.

Your version of Jesus might adhere to your political views. He might justify hating a certain group of people. Your version of Jesus might justify sinful behaviors that scripture clearly speaks to because your version of Jesus is heavy on grace, even if that means He has to be a little squishy on truth.

You might worship a version of Jesus that is willing to mix and match different religious ideals—in the first century, this was known as syncretism ... today it's known as open-mindedness.

Your version of Jesus may have been really firm on certain choices or lifestyles, until someone you love started to struggle with those choices or lifestyles. Now your version of Jesus has changed to accept your loved one's choices or lifestyle.

Your version of Jesus might come down heavily on everyone else's mistakes and yet justify those same behaviors in your life.

Your version of Jesus might justify sin in the name of grace. Or your version of Jesus might justify hate in the name of truth.

These are not the real Jesus. But I don't think the world is nearly as interested in the real Jesus as they are in their ideal version of the son of God.

• • •

My dad said one more thing to me the day I was caught about the fantasy world I was choosing to live in. He told me that the image of that centerfold wasn't real. But he also reminded me there was a real person behind that centerfold—someone who was of great value to God.

I don't know what picture of Jesus you have in your head. I'm guessing it is, at least in part, an airbrushed version of the real thing. But I also know that behind that picture in your head, there is a real Jesus. A real Savior. The son of God. Fully divine. Fully human. Fully in love with you. He's perfect in every way. He loves unconditionally. He calls out sin but still deals out grace. He's better than any version of Jesus we can create, but He won't fit neatly in your perfectly curated life.

Look for that Jesus. The REAL Jesus. Don't settle for a pin-up version.

CHAPTER 3

Swipe Right

Living out the commitments of faith in a world of preference.

The world of dating has changed. I'm old enough (and if you know what I'm talking about, you are as well ... sorry to be the bearer of bad news) to remember the "note."

As a child, I remember the first time I saw a girl and didn't associate her with a direct and very real risk of contracting a case of "the cooties." Slowly but surely, the other boys around me began to change. No longer were they running from girls to avoid this predominant medical threat. Now, they were actually chasing the girls! Imagine! I swore that would never happen to me.

Then one day, it happened to one of my closest friends. I knew something had changed. His shirt was tucked in. He was wearing way too much of what, as an adult, I now know was his dad's Old Spice. He had combed his hair. Something was off.

When we got to recess, he confirmed my suspicions. The chase was on, but he wasn't the one running. He'd become a chaser.

I couldn't understand what was happening! Had all of the boys in my class lost their minds? I doubled down. I swore it would never happen to me. I'd hold strong. And I did. Until I didn't.

One day, there she was. Long blonde hair flowing out from under her little purple beret (that's French for fancy hat). She had pretty eyes and the cutest dimples when she smiled. I know what you're thinking—new girl. And you would be wrong. She had been in my class for several years, and we had sat next to each other all that year. All that time, she was just the girl who sat next to me. And then, almost overnight, that all changed. I changed. She changed.

Suddenly, this girl I had never noticed made me feel sweaty, clammy, and weak in the knees. My heart would race being in the same room with her. I couldn't stop thinking about her. This was it. This was what it felt like. This was LOVE. I was in love.

And that brings me to "the note." During my elementary years, there was only one way to ask a girl to be your girlfriend. No one taught you. Everyone just knew. It's like it was hardwired into the DNA of every prepubescent boy finding his way in the world. I'd seen these notes passed before, but I'd never written one. My hands shook as I wrote those life-changing words in number 2 pencil.

"Will you be my girlfriend?"

Yes No (Circle one)

I remember passing the note to her, palms sweating, hands shaking. I waited for just the right moment when the teacher turned back to the chalkboard (yes I said chalkboard—I told you, I'm old. If you know, you know). Once the teacher's back was turned, I made my move. With one flick of the wrist, I crossed the point of no return and left my romantic future up to fate.

I watched her hide the note under her desk. I sat there nervously as she slowly opened it, one flap at a time. I watched for any evidence of how she was feeling as she read my note and contemplated the two life-changing choices before her. Any tell. Any micro-expressions. She sat there, emotionless, for what seemed like an eternity.

And then, there it was ... at the corner of her mouth. The slightest upturn. The appearance of a dimple. She was smiling. Adrenaline rushed through my body as I watched her pick up her own number 2 pencil and confidently circle "YES."

That's how relationships were established in the 1980s among elementary students (in Sioux Falls, South Dakota, at least). No risk, no reward. There was a cost to putting yourself out there. You were chosen or you weren't. You risked your heart and, at least in our minds, your reputation. But the risk was worth it. Young love was worth it.

When you got older, the note became unacceptable. There was an expectation of actual human interaction. This was early email and before texting. It required, at the very LEAST, a phone call and, more likely, a conversation with a girl who made you so nervous your throat swelled up just thinking about talking to her. The phone call was always risky because there was no guarantee she would answer. It could be her mom or, worse yet, her dad. You never wanted the dad to answer. Talking to her in person was even more risky because what if she rejected you? But again—no risk, no reward.

Today, there is no note. There is often not even a conversation. In 2012, the landscape of dating changed forever. That was the year Tinder launched as a company and gave us an option of "shopping" en masse and based solely on a picture and a digital profile, whether or not to even give a person a chance. No more notes. No more phone calls. All you have to do is swipe right.

• • •

In 2022, medium.com released an article titled "Swipe Right, Swipe Left—but why?" In this article, they trace the establishment of Tinder and the birth of the "swipe right" trend. For those not familiar with this trend, the article defines the terms for us:

> *Swipe right means to like or accept someone, while swipe left means to reject them.*

Acceptance or rejection. Decided by the flick of a wrist and based on nothing more than first impressions. No cost. No consequence. You can dismiss someone before you really ever know them, just because you see something you don't like. The article goes on to make this profound and incredibly sad statement:

> *Swipe left. Swipe right. It's such a small gesture that packs such a big punch.*

Of course it does. It's relationship without the relationship. It's relationship without the risk. *Urban Dictionary* defines swiping right as connecting the word "acceptance" to this transaction.

> *Swipe Right - (verb) A phrase used to describe your acceptance of something. The term was originally a reference to the Tinder app. On Tinder, swiping right means you approve of a male/female after judging them by a few pictures and a short bio. "Swipe right" can be used anytime you make a good choice or approve of something.*

What foundation is a relationship built on when it starts with this mentality? I'm not saying Tinder relationships can't work, and I'm certain many have. But that says more about the quality of the people IN the relationship than it does about the actual process. At its core, the swipe right, swipe left mentality is transforming how we think both about relationships and commitment.

Now, forgive me for making what I feel is a fairly small leap in logic here. I don't claim to have any evidence for my next claim, and certainly nothing that would hold up in court. But I think it will be easy for most to see how I came to this conclusion. Tinder launched in 2012. According to the always reliable and completely accurate online resource known as "Wikipedia," between 2010 and 2020, another trend formed culturally—a trend known as "cancel culture."

> *Cancel culture is a phrase contemporary to the late 2010s and early 2020s used to refer to a culture in which those who are deemed to have acted or spoken in an unacceptable manner are ostracized, boycotted, or shunned ... Those subject to this ostracism are said to have been "canceled."*

Now, I don't consider myself to be the sharpest crayon in the box ... but isn't it possible that a culture that was trained to approach human relationships with a swipe right, swipe right mentality—a culture trained to either accept or reject humans based on simple perception—might have let that thinking bleed into how we approach life in general? If I like it, I accept it. I'll swipe right on that. Don't like it? Get it out of my face. I don't even want to look at it or think about it. I want to swipe left and move on.

And is it also possible that we have maximized our ability to pick and choose what we want to see and what we don't, and we may have inadvertently minimized the fallout of living in such a way? Might it be possible that we aren't fully aware culturally of the cost of outright rejection and of canceling anything we don't like, regardless of whether it may or may not actually be true? Isn't it possible that we may be throwing the proverbial baby out with the bathwater, dismissing unchanging, fundamental truths, just because we don't like them at first glance?

No ... that won't be dangerous at all. (Again, insert heavy sarcasm here.)

• • •

This is ultimately a book on faith. So let's talk about faith for a bit, shall we? Primarily, I want to take a look at the cost of swipe right, swipe left thinking on biblical truth. I don't think anyone would attest or dispute that we are living in a world that is big on acceptance and tolerance. At least it used to be big on tolerance. That eventually wasn't enough. No one wants to just be tolerated. We want more. We want affirmation. Affirmation has become synonymous culturally with love. If you love me, you have to affirm me. If you don't affirm me, you don't love me. There is only one topic I can think of culturally where we are not only NOT expected to be affirming, but we are actually encouraged to be intolerant.

The world is intolerant of Christianity.

I suppose in and of itself, that isn't a fair statement. The world is intolerant of absolutes. Christianity is based on absolutes. It's based on the absolute and unchanging truths of scripture. It's based on the absolute faith we place in Jesus Christ as our only way to eternal life—John 14:6 is clear—Jesus is the way. The only way. The gospel is INCLUSIVE in that Jesus is available to everyone. But it's EXCLUSIVE in that it is based on the absolute truths found in the Bible, and it claims the truth of Jesus is the ONLY truth. It's not your truth or my truth. It's THE truth. The pesky thing about truth claims is that it doesn't feel good when I'm on the other side of that truth.

Do you believe Jesus is the only way to God?

Yes No (Circle one)

More and more in our culture, the answer is NO. Living in a culture that is being shaped at its very core to reject and swipe away anything they don't like has led to more and more people "swiping left" on the absolute truth claims of the Christian faith. And this trend isn't something that is limited to those outside the Christian faith either.

Without question, there are those who are actively rejecting the Christian faith. Typically, the reason for that rejection is tied to an area of life where scripture says "NO" and culture says "YES" or an area where scripture says "YES" and culture says "NO." Any time culture and scripture clash, those opposed to the Christian faith will be quick to dismiss scripture as irrelevant. And why shouldn't they? If you have determined in your life that there is no God, then there's no reason a book Christians claim to believe is the inspired word of a God you don't believe in would have ANY impact on your life. Christians are often disturbed how far culture is from Jesus, but when Jesus isn't your standard and God's word isn't your compass, why would your life not look like this world? It shouldn't surprise us when those who don't claim to believe in Jesus Christ don't look like Jesus Christ.

The far more disturbing trend to me is the reshaping of the church and of Christianity as a whole from within. And by this, I'm not referring to what I believe is the incredibly healthy practice of re-evaluating why we do things the way we do them in the church. I'm talking about what seems to be a church that is living neck deep in a swipe right, swipe left culture that approaches God with this same "pick and choose" mentality.

If you read the Bible and come to the conclusion it truly is the inspired word of God, it will change your life. It has to. If there really is a sovereign and holy creator of the universe ... a God who has existed since before time began and who literally spoke the world into existence, then what He says goes. By virtue of being God, He is the one who gets to determine right and wrong. If God says it's true, it's true. If God says it's right, it's right. If God says it's wrong, it's wrong. It's either that, or He isn't really God.

This is what's known as the sovereignty of God. Sovereignty is defined as a dominant power or supreme authority. For most of us, it can leave a bad taste in our mouths because most, if not all of our human models of sovereignty, are not good, taking the form of monarchies or dictatorships. Ain't nobody got time for that.

Combine this aversion to a supreme authority and to the abuse of supreme power with the cultural rejection of any and all absolutes, and what you end up with is a culture that rejects the notion of God simply due to what God is—an absolute and supreme authority. And what you end up with in the Christian subculture is a bunch of churches full of people who are claiming a devotion to God as their supreme authority but who struggle with authority issues at every turn.

Let me assume for sake of argument that you have read some or all of the Bible. How long did it take you before you read something you didn't like? How long did you read before something in your life crashed hard into a biblical standard and left you with a choice? Let me help you—not long. God is a God of absolutes in a world of anything but. Like it or not, we are all impacted by the culture we live in. You can't live in a culture void of absolutes without getting used to "having it your way."

I believe one of the greatest issues facing the church stems from a culture void of absolutes. Most people who claim to be Christ followers have come to the conclusion God is real. They believe in Jesus. They know we are saved by grace through faith. They have made that decision. But salvation isn't the finish line of faith—it's the starting line. And what most Christians struggle with isn't salvation. It's Lordship.

Does God get to be God in our lives?

Does He get to be sovereign? Does He get to determine what is right and wrong? Does He get to draw the lines? Set the standards? Does He get to determine what is sin and what isn't? Does He get to tell you no? Can He call you to go? These are ultimately Lordship issues and Lordship conversations. No Christian is struggling with Jesus being our Savior. Most Christians seems to be struggling with Jesus being our Lord.

I suspect this is why so many Christians aren't regularly in the word. When you get into His word, you will inevitably experience that collision between your current reality and His divine standards. You will come face to face with godly limitations. You will run smack dab into His sovereign will. You will encounter boundaries you realize you are already crossing and standards it seems like the whole world is ignoring. And you will be the one left with a choice. Something has to move—God or us.

We usually choose us.

Now, before we get too far, let me clarify something in case your ears just perked up. This choice really isn't a choice. God isn't going to move. The real choice is either to align yourself with God or to choose not to. God's not moving His standards for you. He can't be what you want Him to be. He can't be a God of compromise. He can't be less than perfect. He can't be less than holy.

A lot of Christians have given themselves permission to believe God can meet them halfway. I'll give a little, God ... but I need you to give a little, too. So while we follow God's word in many areas of our lives, we also compromise in other areas. When we come up against something in God's word that doesn't work for us, we give ourselves permission to swipe left on those standards, dismissing the parts of His word we don't like. We swipe left on His standards and assume we can still swipe right on Him.

That would be like being on a dating app and swiping right on someone's looks but swiping left on their personality. It doesn't really work that way. It's sort of a package deal. You can't really get one without the other. And neither can you settle for part of God. He is who He is. He is unchanging. He is holy. He is true. He is good. You can't claim to be under the Lordship of Jesus Christ while swiping left on the biblical standards you don't like—standards that He set. Faith is sort of an all or none proposition. You either want Him or you don't.

God is never going to surrender to your will.

Faith is saying "I choose you" even if I don't always like what that means. It's choosing Jesus every day, even when it's hard. As Luke 9:23 reminds us, faith is denying yourself **daily** ... taking up your cross **daily** ... counting the cost **daily** ... and following Him.

I'll be the first to admit—some days I swipe right on Jesus, and some days I swipe left. Romans 12 describes our lives as living sacrifices, holy and acceptable to God. But it says we have to offer ourselves as those sacrifices. We are the ones who have to move, not Him. The problem I have found with a living sacrifice is that it can still crawl off the altar. I never struggle with my salvation. I love Jesus and I love what He has done for me. Where I struggle is to let Him be Lord of my life in all things. It's not because I don't want Jesus. It's because it's hard to count the cost of what that means. It's hard to stand firmly on the absolute truths of the word of God in a world that is actively rejecting Him. It's not hard to be saved by Jesus. It's hard to deny myself daily. But here's a reality we cannot get around when it comes to being a Jesus follower:

Whenever I choose myself, I'm not choosing Him.

If there is any gracious thing about Tinder, it's that it doesn't tell you when someone swipes left on you. If they swipe right, you get a notification they are interested. If they swipe left, if they swipe you out of their lives forever, Tinder graciously lets that disappear into the ether. But when we swipe left on God, He knows. Every. Single. Time. There are some disadvantages to being omniscient. He knows every choice we make that fails to honor Him. He knows every rejection. He knows every compromise. He knows every time we read a truth in His word and think to ourselves, *I'll pass.*

In 2017, Jon Sherwood wrote a blog post titled "Swiping Right on Christ." He writes about how this culture is shifting our perception of what's valuable and beautiful. Christianity is countercultural to this instant gratification, do whatever you feel culture we are living in—but Jesus has always been counterculture. There's no version of following Him that doesn't require this of us. Sherwood calls us to more. He calls us to consider Jesus and all it means to follow and to still swipe right:

> *Ask yourself as a Christian, do you find Christ among the most attractive things in the world? What do you swipe right for over and above him?*

CHAPTER 4

Taking Without Giving

Why pornography (and modern spirituality) are really all about control.

Remember the box? As I look back on my life, I've often asked myself why something I was exposed to before I even fully knew what it was could have such a hold on me for so long. I'd be lying if I didn't admit that at times I can still feel its claws grasping at my life.

Sin is like that. By its very nature, sin can be described as too much of something. It may even be too much of something good. After all, sex and sexuality are an amazing gift created by God with a specific, beautiful, perfect purpose. God gave humanity sex as a gift, with the purpose of both procreation and mutual fulfillment within the confines of marriage. But like he does with all things, the enemy of our souls tempts us with more than what God planned for us.

There's a lot of debate about what constitutes sexual sin. Christians have an annoying habit of trying to make all-inclusive lists—legalistic standards of right and wrong. We'll talk more about this in a bit, but for now, what's important to understand is the WHY behind these lists—control. We think that if we can make a list complete enough and then follow that list, we can control the outcome of our lives. How foolish.

So as to not burden you all with an overwhelming list of what qualifies as sexual sin, let me rather quantify it this way—what is sexual sin? Anything that is MORE. Anything that goes beyond God's plan for sex. In every way, the enemy is trying to get us to make MORE of sex than we ought to.

The world makes sex WAY more important than God's plan in pretty much every way. It's the focus of most music, TV, and movies. Sex is seen by the world as non-negotiable within the context of any relationship—from dating to engagement to cohabitation to marriage. Sex is seen less as a gift for marriage and more as a rite of passage for all humanity. Our sexuality is made to be more, as culture blends sexuality with our very identity. God up in heaven is whispering to us constantly in His still, small voice, "this is not ALL you are—YOU are so much MORE than just your sexuality." But His voice is swallowed up by images, ads, conversations, entertainment, and cultural norms that are all shouting the same thing—"this is who you are." This is all you are.

The pornography is a multi-billion (yes, with a B) dollar a year industry, seen as a tool to help stimulate sexual relationships and also a replacement for those who struggle to find real human relationships—because, after all, no one can live without sexual fulfillment. This is why the box held so much sway in my life. It wasn't just about temptation (though there was plenty of that). This was about identity. I wrongly believed I was more of a man in those hidden moments. And I wrongly believed I was in control of ... I don't even know what. I kept going back to the box looking for a feeling of power. Every time I went back, it promised more but offered less. Yet in my insanity (isn't that what it's called when you try the same thing over and over and expect different results?), I kept going back to the box, looking for different answers in the same place. Eventually, the box wasn't enough—I needed more. And I found it. It's everywhere. Pretty soon, I wasn't coming when the opportunity arose. I had to create opportunities. Pornography gave me the illusion of relationship and the illusion of control. In reality, I had neither, there was no real relationship, and it wasn't me that was in control.

Eventually, I got old enough for real relationships. With real girls. Real people. Daughters. Future mothers. Children of the King. But I didn't always treat them that way. Sometimes I brought the expectations pornography had given me into the human relationship. We searched for intimacy but instead found regret, shame, and hurt. Other times, I gave up on the "human" part of the relationship and settled instead for the images I could control. So much easier. All the benefits, none of the expectations. Sounds great, right? At least it did to a young teenage boy. How little I knew.

At the end of the day, the control pornography offered me wasn't real because the relationship wasn't real. Real relationships aren't something you can control or manipulate. They are the essence of vulnerability. Perhaps that's why so many real relationships struggle—we are all fighting for control. Every one of us knows someone who has experienced the ugly side of relationships. Divorce. Abuse. Manipulation. Control.

If you really think about it, any time abuse is present, it will be within the context of a one-sided relationship. Whether we're talking physical, mental, or emotional abuse, or even abandonment—abuse only happens when one side takes control of the relationship in some way and it is no longer about two; now it's about one. It's no longer about us; now it's about me. In fact, I'll be bold enough as to go further with my statement:

One-sided relationships are always abusive.

I'm blessed to be a part of a marriage that is defined by mutual submission. We are in this together. We are in it for each other. I mourn all the couples who don't know what I know in my marriage. But there was a season, particularly early, where we were both guilty of relational abuse. And there was a season where, if I'm honest, my approach to our marriage was about me, and I was definitely guilty of abuse. And if you're married, and you're honest, you've actually been there, too.

Culturally, we are hardwired for self-protection. Marriage is designed by God to completely undo that natural tendency. In marriage, you will either discover how to humble yourself, or you will have a marriage that either fails or that fails to ever be what God designed it to be.

In the Bible, in Paul's letter to the Ephesian church, he lays out some of the most famous words ever penned on marriage. And it might actually be more fitting to call this scripture passage "infamous," as it has not always been embraced by hearers. The full passage is found in Ephesians 5:21-33 (I encourage you to pause here and go read it). I want to draw our attention to a specific part of the passage and to a key word—a dirty word—in the eyes of most of the world. SUBMIT.

> [22] *For wives, this means submit to your husbands as to the Lord.* [23] *For a husband is the head of his wife as Christ is the head of the church. He is the Savior of his body, the church.* [24] *As the church submits to Christ, so you wives should submit to your husbands in everything. (Ephesians 5:22-24 NLT)*

HOLD THE PHONE. There is no room in a world that is fighting for equal rights for a scripture like that! I am married to an amazing, godly woman who would be the very first to admit she struggles with this word! Now, if you continue to read in Ephesians 5, you'd end up reading a whole lot about the guy's part of this deal. As a man who strives to live this out in my marriage, I can tell you—it ain't no picnic. But really, the key verse in this whole passage is found in verse 21:

> *And further, submit to one another out of reverence for Christ. (Ephesians 5:21 NLT)*

Every piece of this is critical. If you haven't figured it out yet, this is a low-key book on holiness. I'm going to be getting to that point and that agenda here shortly. But you can't miss this. EVERY part of this verse is critical.

- **Submit** - A choice to lay your own rights down for another.
- **One Another** - Both parties have to make the same choice.
- **For Christ** - If you don't start here, you'll never submit.

One of my greatest mentors in life has been Pastor Kevin Myers, founding Pastor of 12 Stone Church in Atlanta, Georgia. Kevin has taught me more about life, leadership, and ministry than almost anyone else on this planet. Kevin had a term he would always apply to this passage and to this concept of relationship.

Mutual Voluntary Submission.

Kevin speaks of mutual voluntary submission as being willing to take a knee ... or two if needed, in submission to one another out of love. According to Kevin, the idea of submitting is a revolutionary concept in a world filled with people who are trying to get everyone else to submit to their will and their way.

In his book *The Second Happy*, Kevin had this to say about this idea of MVS:

> *The idea behind mutual voluntary submission is about more than humbly yielding to another person. It is an expression of living in reverence to Jesus. When you revere Christ first and foremost, you follow his guidelines for making your marriage work.*

According to Kevin, it takes all THREE of these things to "tango" as they say. It's mutual in that it takes both of us. It's voluntary in that it's a choice. It's submission in that we each put the other first. It's simple. It's profound. It's powerful. It's impossible without Jesus. None of this is possible without reverence for Christ. As is so often in the kingdom of God, things are simple, but that doesn't mean they are easy. God's plan and will for our lives is both incredibly simple (not complex) and incredibly difficult (not easy). And yet, they are without question the most important things. I love how Kevin summarizes these thoughts:

> *Few things in life are more powerful than a voluntary sacrifice. It's an expression of real love that towers over our culture's silly definitions of love. Our culture exhibits a self-serving love rooted in childish wants, indulgent pleasures, dysfunctional co-dependence, or sullen willfulness. Real love makes sacrifices for the other person.*

This kind of sacrifice is only possible through the power of God's Spirit in our lives. And this kind of power can only be found in a reverential and loving relationship with Jesus Christ. It's my belief that the reason so many of us struggle to submit to one another in our human relationships is because we lack reverence for Christ. Until we get that relationship right, our other relationships don't really stand a chance.

One-sided relationships are abusive because they are always about taking without giving.

Pornography is a one-sided relationship. Honestly, it's a struggle to even call it a relationship. In fact, I don't even think most people who are currently involved with using and addicted to pornography would themselves call it a relationship.

And yet all the time, Christians approach this real and true relationship offered to us by our heavenly Father as anything but a real relationship. When it comes to our faith, I think most Christians are one-sided in their relationship with God. This is the real difference between salvation and Lordship. If all you are getting from this relationship with God is salvation, your relationship with God is one-sided. Relationships, real relationships, are always both give and take. If Jesus is your Savior but not your Lord, you are taking without giving. By our definition, this is spiritually abusive.

In Christian circles, I see two forms of one-sided relationship. Both are less than God wants. Both are more about how we view God and our relationship with Him than they are about anything else. Keep in mind, relationships are by definition two-sided. Yet both of these viewpoints focus on one side of this relationship.

Viewpoint #1: It's all about God.

Now, I know what you're thinking, and yes, it kind of is all about God. It's all about what God, through His son, Jesus Christ, has done for us. And yet what I am talking about here is the viewpoint many Christians struggle with that leads to legalism, and that makes Christianity feel like an unbearable weight of religion rather than a transformational relationship. For so many Christians, it's all about God in that God is the one who always takes but never gives. And this leads us to the first of two critical theological ideas.

God is transcendent.

God is bigger. God is beyond. This is all about the "other-ness" of God. The website, vocabulary.com, defines transcendence in such a powerful way:

> *Transcendent describes something so excellent that it's beyond the range of human understanding.*

Without question, this is what God is. It's not all God is, but it definitely describes God. He is so excellent, it is beyond the realm of understanding. Seeing God this way is an incredibly positive thing. The picture of God as outlined in the Old Testament is a God who is unapproachable. He is so holy, even saying His name was not allowed—it was too holy to cross the lips of a human. The temple system pointed to His holiness. When we look around the world today and see beautiful cathedrals, amazing works of art, powerful pieces of sacred music, what we are seeing is man's attempt to point to the transcendence of God.

Where this viewpoint becomes dangerous is when we ONLY see God this way. The Pharisees and religious leaders of the New Testament struggled with Jesus because they saw God as one-dimensional, and they saw their relationship with Him as one-sided. They made up rules to help them follow God's rules so that they were never at risk of being on the wrong side of a God who was supposed to deliver them but who they certainly weren't assuming loved them. They are often accused of missing the heart of God, probably because they were unaware God had a heart.

I watch so many Christians today who do everything they

do in their faith to keep God from being mad at them. They go through the motions of faith to appease God. Their viewpoint of God is not one of grace and mercy and love but of a God who takes but who does not give. It's often a relationship driven by our fear of a God who can send us to hell and not of a God who sent His son to save us from that fate. One-sided relationships are always abusive. In this version of Christianity, God is, in essence, the abuser ... which allows us to play the role of the victims.

You may wonder why anyone would choose to view God this way, particularly when scripture is so full of God's unfailing love. The answer is simple—control. This relationship isn't fun. It's not fulfilling. It isn't meaningful. But it makes my faith manageable.

When it comes to legalism, the thrill is found in being in control of my FAITH.

If God is only transcendent, then He is not only big, He's far away. I can keep Him at arm's length. I can make my lists, then follow them. I can surround myself with things that remind me how big God is but never feel obligated to make God part of my day to day. I can fill my life with religious things at pre-scheduled times, but I feel no obligation to get to know God—what a ridiculous notion—He's GOD! Faith is about doing the right thing, following the rules. It's about getting baptized. Getting confirmed. Checking all the boxes. It's about putting on my best face. Because God is to be feared. I do not love Him. But I fear Him.

Viewpoint #2: It's all about Me.

In ancient Israel, the idea of me was a foreign concept. Faith was never about "me." It was always about "we." It was about "us." There was no such thing in Jewish cultural understanding as the idea of a personal relationship with God. It's a concept that wouldn't even have made sense to them, and it's one of the things that caused the religious leaders to struggle so much with Jesus.

Today in the church, we almost exclusively talk about your personal relationship with God. We are obsessed with the idea of each person accepting Jesus as "Your personal Lord and Savior." And we should be. The idea that God doesn't just love US ... He loves ME—it's compelling to say the least. In a world where every single religion on the planet is about earning your way save one—the fact that God wants a relationship with me is the single greatest factor setting Christianity apart. In no way will I minimize this incredible and powerful truth. And yet this, too, can be taken too far. And this leads to our second theological idea.

God is immanent.

God is close. He is personal. He is near. Here, we turn to Merriam Webster for a definition:

> *Immanent (in the context of religion) is "being within the limits of possible experience or knowledge."*

If transcendence is all about God's limitlessness, immanence makes the idea of God manageable. This is John 3:16 in a nutshell. "God so loved the world, that He sent Jesus FOR US."

Again, this is all about extremes. Again, the power of knowing God isn't just powerful, He's close—I can't tell you what this has done for my faith. Without question, the God of the universe is longing for a relationship with you. But again, the danger is when this is the ONLY way you see God. In Romans 6, Paul has to write to warn Christians—God's grace isn't an excuse to keep sinning. Their attitude was "Jesus paid the price so that I can do whatever I want."

Today, I think there are so many Christians who are only in this relationship with God to take what God is offering but with no plan of giving any of themselves in return. And why shouldn't they? They've grown up with dating apps and social media platforms offering relationships that are completely one-sided and cost you nothing. They have a picture of God as a God who gives, but He doesn't expect anything in return. They use grace to justify and prop up all kinds of lifestyles. They disregard scriptures that directly speak against certain sins or that expect us to conform our lifestyle to His standards because, in their viewpoint, a God who loves me would never expect me to give up that thing to change who I am.

But that's exactly what He expects.

The false belief of so many contemporary Christians is that God is a God of grace ... period. God is good. Jesus is my homeboy. God is a God of love—He loves me just as I am and doesn't expect me to change anything in my life. The word for this is license.

When it comes to license, the thrill is found in being in control of my CHOICES.

The only problem with this view of life, or of faith for that matter, is what happens any time we are in control of our own choices. Humanity does not have a great track record of decision-making when left in control. And I don't even have to know you to know that any time you have been left fully in charge of the choices, something went off the rails. Somewhere you justified too much. Somewhere you excused too much.

Both of these are pictures of faith as a one-sided relationship. The reason I have titled this book *Jesus be the Centerfold* is because the parallel rings so true on every level. What God is longing for with each of us is a relationship. And what God brings to the relationship is all of Himself—both His transcendent glory and His immanent closeness. God wants to bring all of Himself to us, and He wants all of us in return. Give and take. This is the nature of a real relationship.

We are being offered a real relationship. With the real God. Creator. Sustainer. Savior. Friend. Sometimes we bring the expectations of this life to the relationship. In life, we've searched for intimacy but instead found regret, shame, and hurt. We're afraid God may hurt us, too. There is a fear of true intimacy that keeps us settling for less. Instead of embracing all of who God is and instead of surrendering ourselves fully to His Lordship, we settle for a one-sided version of relationship that we can control. So much easier. All the benefits, none of the expectations. It sounds great. It always falls short.

Let's go back to Ephesians 5 for a moment together. Why does God love this picture of marriage so much? We see it all over the pages of scripture. God even goes as far as to describe the church as His bride. God is painting a picture for us. Think about it this way: What would it look like to have an Ephesians 5 relationship with God the Father?

If the church is meant to be the bride of Christ, then our call should be to submit ourselves to God in all we do. Everything.

Christ, as our bridegroom, has already sacrificed everything for us. But what's astounding is what it means for verse 21 to be true in this relationship as well. Let's look at it again:

> *And further, submit to one another out of reverence for Christ. (Ephesians 5:21 NLT)*

Is it possible in the relationship God is desiring with us, He is just as willing to submit all of Himself to us as He wants us to be to submit all of ourselves to Him? God desires a relationship with His church. When you put your faith in Him, you are committing to that relationship. You aren't just accepting His gift of salvation. You're also choosing to submit yourself to His Lordship in your life. He wants a relationship where you give all of yourself to Him and where He gives all of Himself to you through Jesus. He wants a relationship where He is both transcendent and all-powerful, and where He is immanent, walking daily with you through every circumstance in your life. He wants a relationship that is give and take.

When it comes to surrender, the thrill is found in LETTING GO of control.

John Bevere, in his book *The Awe of God*, summarizes the wonder of a relationship with God that actually costs you something ... a relationship where God is not only close but is also allowed to be God:

> *Here's a firm truth: you will never find God's wonderful presence in an atmosphere where He's not revered and held in awe.*

May we never settle for a God we can control. May we never settle for God's presence or His wonder. Father gives us both. Give us all of yourself. And take all of us in return.

CHAPTER 5

Lust v. Love

How "falling in love" has redefined love forever.

I LOVE ... well ... LOVE. I'm, without question, a romantic at heart. When I fell, I fell hard. I'm guilty of producing more than my fair share of "mixtapes" for girls I liked. I secretly liked the romantic movies my mom and sisters would watch ... okay ... maybe not so secretly. I've rented limos for girls for special occasions, written poetry, composed original songs, driven thirty minutes across town for just ten minutes with a girl ... multiple times. And late at night in the 1980s and '90s, if you listened very carefully, you would have heard the soulful crooning of Boyz II Men, Chicago, Air Supply, and a whole host of early "rat pack" style crooners from Sinatra to Tony Bennet. Yup ... I was that guy.

I LOVE ... LOVE.

Or at least the idea of it. The older I've gotten, the more I've wrestled with the language we use to describe this thing called love. Terms like "falling in love" and "love at first sight" that used to ring so true at a soul level for me now fall flat in my much expanded universe. It took experiencing real love—love borne of sacrifice and love that came at a cost—to realize just how hollow the promises that ideas like falling in love really ring.

At this point in my life, I don't believe in falling in love. I don't believe in love at first sight. It's strange for me to admit that, as in the same breath, I admit that I love Hallmark movies. I soak in the predictability of a perfect Christmas and a true love story that develops over the long weekend. I can't help it. I can't get enough.

And yet, even watching it, I know what I'm seeing isn't real. I mean, love is real ... no question. And YES, I do believe people can meet each other and just "know." My in-laws are living proof that you can meet in a moment, write letters for a while, marry after a handful of months, and commit to each other for a lifetime. And that's the key word.

Commit.

Any relationship can be defined by love. But no relationship becomes a loving one without commitment. What started as a feeling with my in-laws very quickly became a choice, a DAILY choice, to love. My wife and I were friends for a while before we dated, but when we started dating, I knew at that moment I was going to marry her. We were engaged within two months. We were at the mall, and some of our friends were trying on wedding rings for fun (it was a late-1990s thing—don't judge). Steph tried on a ring, and when I saw her face, I purchased the ring on the spot.

The thing is ... I hadn't proposed yet.

Steph looked at me with surprise, sprinkled with both a lot of excitement and a quite a bit of shock. When she asked me what I was doing, I said confidently, "I know I'm gonna marry you! Don't you know you're gonna marry me?" I didn't have to hesitate. I didn't have to wait. I knew. Yes, I knew I loved her. Yes, I knew she was amazing and out of my league. But that's not what I knew that day. I could confidently buy that ring because I knew I was ready to **choose** her, and to keep choosing her.

The reason I could know this so clearly was because this wasn't the first wedding ring I'd purchased. It was actually the second. Or at least I ALMOST purchased it. I had dated the same girl for a long time in high school. She loved me so much. She had made her choice. She was in. She was willing to count the cost. The only problem is, I wasn't. I told myself I was. I told myself that lie often. I told myself enough that I convinced myself to purchase a ring. But there was always hesitation in my heart.

It wasn't that I didn't have feelings for her or even care deeply about her. I did, and I actually still do. She was one of my best friends in the world. I have so many amazing memories growing up with her and a group of close-knit compadres. I did feel love for her. I thought I was ready to make the choice. Time would prove that wasn't the case.

I'll never forget the moment God told me I had to let her go. I was heartbroken. But what struck me more is that I wasn't devastated. I could imagine life without her. Love ... or rather the choice to love ... is more than that. Looking back, there were signs. That first time around, I put the ring on layaway. I made payments over time. I asked what the return policy was if something went wrong. With Stephani, I financed that baby on the spot as a poor college student. I found a way to make every payment. I worked extra hours to afford it. We walked out that day with the ring. I looked at it twenty times a day until the day I actually proposed. I couldn't wait to give it to her. To express my love. To express to her—**I choose you.** That, my friends, is what love looks like.

And more critically, it's what love continues to look like. I'd like to say our marriage has always felt the best—five stars and two enthusiastic thumbs up every day. That would be a lie. Marriage vows feel like throw-away comments when you're making them, but they mean business. For better or worse? In sickness and health? For richer or poorer? You make those promises thinking you will always be only on the upside of those promises. Always better. Always healthy. Never poor. We have been married since 2001, and we have experienced all of the above, both the ups and the downs. There are days when feelings are enough to carry your love. There are other days where love costs you everything you have to give and more. That's the nature of love.

And that's why I don't believe in love at first sight. That's why I don't think you can "fall in love." Love is a choice made in a moment and proven over a lifetime. And biblical love, as we will talk about in a bit, is the deepest love of them all.

And yet we have all experienced those feelings. Being swept off our feet. Getting weak in the knees. Feeling butterflies in our stomach. Being struck by someone's beauty. Most of the movie and music industry is built on songs describing this type of love. I can't deny the feelings I had when I passed that note to that first girl all those years ago. I can't deny that I have literally been so struck by just the sight of someone that I can't stop thinking about them. If that's not love, what is it?

I propose this not as someone isolated from reality but as someone who has experienced too much of it in a lot of ways. I speak as someone who has been there and done that when it comes to all of these feelings. Need I remind you—Boyz II Men? Air Supply? I have been smitten, enamored, over the moon, enchanted, infatuated, and under the spell. All of the above. Check, check, and double check. But I don't think I was in love.

I think I was in lust.

Lust v. Love

This may startle you, as culture and the use of words in culture often give a connotation to words that, while accurate at times, was never intended to become the sole way to think about a word. Lust carries with it a set of very coarse or foul mental images. When words have been used and abused by culture, it's always good to go back to the original definitions, in Webster's Dictionary circa 1913. Here's what ole' Webster had to say way back then:

> Lust: *To have an eager, passionate, and especially an inordinate or sinful desire, as for the gratification of the sexual appetite or of covetousness;*

This is how I think most of the world defines love. Eager. Passionate. A feeling. A desire. We don't call it sinful. We don't like that world. And we don't call it sex, either. It's intimacy. We are guilty of replacing and redefining these words we don't like, and as a result, we have replaced and redefined love.

This is why we think we can fall in love. And out of it, for that matter. Because slowly but surely, real love has been usurped. And in its place is a disappointing substitute. We don't fall in love. We fall in lust. Lust is temporary. It is feelings driven. It's haphazard. It comes and goes. It ebbs and flows. It has led us culturally to a 50% divorce rate, an increased rate of cohabitation, and a completely broken idea of love.

If you've read this far in the book, you know I'm a total Jesus guy. I'm all in. And what the Bible tells us is that Jesus is all about love. In fact, take that thought one step further. According to the Bible, God isn't just loving. God IS love. The most quoted verse in scripture, a verse known by church goers and non-church goers alike, is John 3:16:

> *For this is how God loved the world: He gave his one and only Son, so that everyone who believes in him will not perish but have eternal life.* (John 3:16 NLT)

Other translations of the Bible translate the opening phrase, "For God SO loved the world." That's what God does. He loves. He loves unconditionally. He loves sacrificially. But He loves according to a different definition of love than I think the world understands. I hear so many people talk angrily about God, claiming a loving God couldn't send people to hell. They ask me to explain how that can happen. How can a God of love actually send people to hell? The answer is simple really:

He doesn't.

One of the most amazing and beautiful things about love is that love is a choice. God loves you. But you do not have to choose to love Him back. The mere idea that a sovereign, all-powerful God, who created the universe just by speaking, would make the choice to give us ... well, a choice ... it's beyond what I can really fully comprehend. It is, without question, the single greatest act of love this world has ever known. And it's an act of love punctuated by the death of Jesus on the cross—a cross He willingly went to—so we could have this choice. What love.

That God, the one who loves you so profoundly and so deeply, doesn't send anyone to hell. He doesn't send anyone anywhere. He simply gives us that critical thing that real love always requires. Choice. We can choose Him. We can reject Him. We can deny Him. It's up to us. The only thing we can't do is have it both ways. And really, isn't that the nature of love? Isn't that part of what makes love what it is?

When I married Stephani, I made a choice. Every day, I choose her again and again. Some days, that's easy. Other days, less so. And it has to be hard for her to return the favor on most days! I have the freedom any day I want to wake up and to NOT choose her. I can give up. Walk out. End the relationship. There is a path that goes with that choice. She won't force that path upon me.

If I chose to be done, I would be choosing a different path than the one I am currently on. She isn't holding me captive. We are living in love, which means we are freely choosing each other every single day. Day by day. And any time I wanted, I could make another choice. And so could she. What I can't do, however, is have it both ways. That's just the nature of love. I'm either in or I'm out. But I can't be both.

When we want all the benefits of God's love in our lives and yet don't want the requirements that go with being in a love relationship with our Savior, that's wanting it both ways. I can't tell you how many people I talk to who are angry at God because they think it's unreasonable for Him to expect from humanity what He does. It's unfair, they claim. They are angry because of His expectation that we would actually love Him back.

How dare He.

I think one of the greatest reasons we struggle with the idea of a love relationship with God is because we approach the conversation with very different definitions of love. What God is inviting us into and what we think this relationship will look like are fundamentally different. When pastors preach the gospel, inviting people into this love relationship with Jesus, we have a tendency to camp in God's grace, which, without question, is beyond amazing. And yet we tend to focus on all the benefits of this relationship—things like forgiveness, eternal life, and the washing away of our sins. What we often fail to mention, however, is our part of this love relationship. We talk about God's beautiful and undeserved commitment to us. Rarely do we talk about our commitment to Him. But no relationship is one-sided.

I've performed a lot of weddings over the years. So many I've actually lost count. One thing I tell almost every couple is that it takes two to enter this covenant relationship. It only takes one to break it. All it takes for a marriage to fail is for one person to refuse to hold up their end of the marriage commitment. Everyone says they understand this. But if they did, we wouldn't see so many marriages end in divorce. Often people will list "irreconcilable differences" as the reason for their divorce. In reality, any differences are reconcilable if both parties are committed to the relationship. What is really happening is that one, or both, party has irreconcilable commitment issues.

This is often the mentality we bring into this conversation about a relationship with God. He wants a love relationship where we both lay ourselves down for each other—Him for us and us for Him. And honestly, I think most people who pursue a faith relationship with God want that, too. But again, we are working from very different definitions of love. So I've been beating around the bush, tip-toeing around an idea for about three pages now. So I'm just going to come out and say it.

I think we are in lust with God.

Even writing that just now made me cringe a little bit, partly because of my aversion to the idea of lust and partly because, honestly, I really believe what I just said.

I think most people who engage in this whole gospel conversation about God's love for us think what we are experiencing is love. We hear the church talking about how much God loves us. About how all we have to do is believe. That it's by grace we are saved through faith in Jesus Christ. There's nothing we have to do. He's offering us a free gift—we just have to choose to receive it. We hear about how if we confess our sins, God is faithful and just to forgive us and to cleanse us of all unrighteousness. We read about God's unfailing, never-ending, unconditional love for us. We are told that His mercies are new every morning. And every single word of this is true! And hearing this amazing news makes us feel all kinds of wonderful emotions. It's easy to become overwhelmed by God's amazing grace. We love the idea that God loves us so much.

But what we often fail to do is to consider what loving Him back might mean.

Every girl that ever gave me butterflies in my stomach is now in the rearview mirror of my life. Every girl except one. My wife. The one I committed to. The one relationship where I counted the cost. The one I chose.

In all those other relationships, things could have been great. I definitely **felt** very in love with all these girls. But as I got to know them and as the relationship progressed, I realized there were expectations that went with this connection. I loved the idea of being in love with these girls. I didn't love what that actually looked and felt like. I didn't love that they actually had expectations for me. And with a growing realization of the cost of these relationships, there was a diminishing feeling of excitement. Anticipation was replaced by obligation. And I realized something in each and every one of these situations. I loved the idea of these relationships. But I didn't love the actual relationships. When the butterflies were gone, so was my commitment.

This, I think, is where most Christians find themselves if they are willing to be completely honest. When we got into this thing, we were swept off our feet by the idea of a Savior who went to the cross and shed His blood for our salvation. We had all these pictures of being rescued from the mess we made of our lives. In ways eerily similar to the biblical Israelites, we pictured Jesus as a shining knight on a white steed coming to sweep us off our feet. Imagine our surprise when the knight climbs not off a bleached charger but a donkey. And when we get a closer look, He turns out to be a man. A common man. A carpenter. And when He starts preaching, He isn't talking about saving me **for** this life but **from** it. The biggest problems, He claims, aren't the ones in the world around me. They are the sins in the heart within me. **This is not what I expected at all.**

I think what most of the church has found is that while they were in love with the **idea** of Jesus, they might not actually be in love with Him. Shaped by the paper mache version of love we have grown up with, so many spiritual seekers have "fallen for" Jesus and for His beautiful message of grace. And boy, do I get that. Grace is the thing that sets Christianity apart from every other religion. (That and having a real Savior, who rose from the dead, conquered sin and death, and now sits at the right hand of God the Father, interceding on our behalf ... but I digress ...)

But what people often do not take account of is the relational nature of the gospel of Jesus Christ. Put in terms we are familiar with, love takes two. The pages of scripture describe a God who loved us so much that He sent His son, Jesus Christ, to be the perfect sacrifice. They describe a God who has gone to incredible lengths to redeem humanity and has been incredibly patient with a people who, for the most part, overlook Him. Some would say, "If He's an all-powerful God, why doesn't He just fix it?" Hasn't God learned yet that humanity is just gonna mess it up? Every. Single. Time. The Bible is nothing if not a story of a lost, helpless, hopeless, and endlessly belligerent species. As the psalmist so aptly put it in Psalm 8, "Who are we God, that you should even notice us?" If God knows we are so helpless and hopeless, why hasn't He just intervened and fixed it all? Why?

Because love takes two.

The relationship God is looking for with humanity is one based on love and defined by choice. Yes, the Bible is a book describing God's incredible love and patience for the human race. But it is also a book outlining our part. It's filled with God's expectations for us. It's clear about what God is longing for from His people. As with any relationship, this thing comes with expectations.

In fact, when asked what the greatest commandment in all of the scriptures is, Jesus gave a two-part answer:

> [37] *Jesus replied, "You must love the Lord your God with all your heart, all your soul, and all your mind.'* [38] *This is the first and greatest commandment.* [39] *A second is equally important: 'Love your neighbor as yourself.'* [40] *The entire law and all the demands of the prophets are based on these two commandments."* (Matthew 22:37-40 NLT)

This is a compilation of two Old Testament verses. The first is found in a passage every Jew not only knew but quoted as a life verse every day. It's in a passage known as the Shema (which just means "hear"). In Deuteronomy 6:5, we find what every Jew would have considered the "right answer" to the question about the greatest commandment.

Love God.

Love the Lord your God with all that you are. This was, for a Jewish person, the definition of faith. But Jesus, in this moment in the New Testament, forever attaches a second, much less well-known scripture to the greatest commandment. In essence, He is claiming the greatest commandment is both these things. Not one. Both. Together. Always. The second passage is found in Leviticus 19:18. The command we find here?

Love people.

All people. While the passage refers to our neighbor, if you keep reading, you find out quickly that Jesus' plan was for this to apply much broader than your apartment building or cul-de-sac. How broad? Well ... everyone. Like ... EVERYONE. Jesus says that in all of scripture, there is no commandment that doesn't come back to these two. Love God. Love others. God's greatest command to humanity is about love. And not the flimsy Valentine card definition of love. Jesus is calling us to a love almost exclusively defined by Him and almost only found in the pages of scripture.

Agape. Agapao.

This work is originally a greek word- **ἀγάπη** (agápē). dictionary.com defines this word as unconditional, sacrificial love.

Did you hear that language? Unconditional. Sacrificial. It's easy to think of God's love for us this way. After all, He is an unconditional God. And Jesus died a sacrificial death on the cross. Regardless of your faith level in these statements, it's not a stretch to apply them to God. But Jesus is using this same word for love to describe God's greatest commandment for humanity. This is God's command ... for us. Love God unconditionally and sacrificially. Love others unconditionally and sacrificially as you love yourself unconditionally and sacrificially.

The website, dictionary.com, goes on to say that agape is the kind of love that is felt by a person that causes them to be willing to do anything for the other person, without expecting anything in return. It's the love that causes everyday heroes to jump into the water even though they can't swim to save a drowning person they don't even know. It's the love that drives selfless individuals to donate part of their kidney to a stranger they happen to be a match with. Agape is the driving force behind the first responders who ran back into the Twin Towers on 9/11 for people they didn't even know. Their names are forever etched in black marble at the site of their heroism in New York City in large part because of agape.

So in a sense, you could say the potential for agape lurks

inside every one of us. Which makes sense, as we are all created in the image of the one who doesn't just love but who is, in His very nature, agape. And yet it seems impossible when I think about my everyday life. Heroism in a moment is amazing and commendable. But life is made up of a lot of moments. And the world is full of a lot of people. And most of them are, moment by moment, pretty darn unlovable.

But let's take this one step further. Jesus is asked—what is the greatest commandment? His answer? **Love God the way God loves you. Love others the way God loves them**. That's what God wants the most. Let's look at just a few examples from scripture. In 1 John 4, we read about God's desire for us to love this world the way He loves the world.

> [7] *Dear friends, let us continue to love one another, for love comes from God. Anyone who loves is a child of God and knows God.* [8] *But anyone who does not love does not know God, for God is love.*
>
> [9] *God showed how much he loved us by sending his one and only Son into the world so that we might have eternal life through him.* [10] *This is real love—not that we loved God, but that he loved us and sent his Son as a sacrifice to take away our sins.* [11] *Dear friends, since God loved us that much, we surely ought to love each other.* (1 John 4:7–11 NLT)

There's that pesky word again, splashed all over the pages of 1 John. Let us continue to agape one another. God is agape. If we don't agape, we don't know God, for God is agape.

God is love. God is not butterflies in the stomach. He's not a swooning or weak in the knees feeling. He is unconditional, sacrificial love. And those who call ourselves Christians and label our lives with the name of His son—we are called to love like He loves. 1 Corinthians 13 is often used at weddings, but it's not even originally a wedding passage. It's part of a letter written to a church by the Apostle Paul because they were struggling to get this whole "love one another" thing right. It's a description of the love God desires and demands from those who claim the name of His son.

> [4] *Love is patient and kind. Love is not jealous or boastful or proud* [5] *or rude. It does not demand its own way. It is not irritable, and it keeps no record of being wronged.* [6] *It does not rejoice about injustice but rejoices whenever the truth wins out.* [7] *Love never gives up, never loses faith, is always hopeful, and endures through every circumstance.* (1 Corinthians 13:4-7 NLT)

I'd be hard-pressed to point to any marriages, mine included, where both spouses are keeping this commandment perfectly. And yet this is the love God is calling us to offer to every person that we encounter. That's impossible without an act of ... well ... God! As it turns out, the only thing that makes it possible to love people this unconditionally and sacrificially is when we love God this unconditionally and sacrificially, and as part of that relationship, His Spirit actually takes up residence in us and does the heavy lifting for us.

I'd like to say, as I look at God's church across the United States, I could say, "Yup ... I see it." In truth, most Christians I know don't look or act like they are in love with God at all. They look like a bunch of people who are on the back side of a summer crush. The excitement is gone, the joy is drained from their eyes, and they are just looking for an excuse. People walk away when hard times come as if God didn't keep his promise. They blame God for not being loving. They claim He didn't keep up His end of the deal.

Um ... the cross. Yeah, He did his part.

When God said He so loved the world, He made the conditions pretty clear. I'm all in on you if you're all in on me. He didn't promise us things would be easy. He promised to love us enough to never leave us or forsake us. Is it so strange for Him to expect the same thing in return?

If you're a Christian, are you in love with Jesus? Are you daily denying yourself, taking up your cross and following Him? Are you choosing agape every day, even the days that are hard? Are you offering an unconditional and sacrificial love to those you meet every day? Or did you just lust after the idea of salvation and eternal life? The God of this universe knows you by name. He saw you before you were born. He knows the number of hairs on your head. He collects every one of your tears in a bottle. He knows all the greatest things about you that make you so wonderful and unique. And He knows all the worst things about you—all your mistakes, flaws, imperfections, hidden sins, and regrets. And just as you are, God agapes you. He is unconditional and sacrificially in love with you. So much so that His greatest command, the thing all of scripture hangs on, is this:

Love me back. Don't fall for me. Choose me.

CHAPTER 6

Prostituting the Church

Turning the greatest love the world has ever known into a transaction.

My wife and I love documentaries ... or a more accurate way of saying it would be "My wife loves documentaries ... and I love my wife." As a result, we watch quite a few documentaries together (and she watches even more of them without me). It's not the topic that is as important as the story. My wife wants to know the story behind the history. She's not only after the facts—she wants all the feelings as well.

As a result of this desire to know and to feel history, we've watched documentaries on a very broad and eclectic selection of topics. We've seen the war documentaries by renowned documentarian, Ken Burns. We've also watched documentaries on the making of candy. I don't know who that one was by. We've watched documentaries on everything from the settling of the Wild West to the story of the world's most prolific serial killers. Like I said, a broad and eclectic selection.

One of our favorite short documentaries is the *Made Us* series, particularly *The Movies That Made Us*. These documentaries take a behind-the-scenes look in just under an hour at the stories and details behind the making of some of the most well-known films of all time, from *Home Alone* to *Elf* and from *Robocop* to *Friday the 13th*.

Recently, we watched the story about the making of *Pretty Woman*. This was a unique tale of a well-known actor (Richard Gere) and an unknown at this point actress (Julia Roberts), who play a corporate raider, and, of all things, a prostitute. What makes the story of the making of this film so interesting is that it is, ultimately, a Disney film. Touchstone Pictures (the non-animated arm of Disney filmmaking) took a major risk telling this story. At the time this film was made (1990), Disney still had a reputation as wholesome, kid-friendly entertainment. And yet Disney was so enamored with this story, they took the risk of making a movie where a prostitute was not only a main character but ends up being the heroine and the romantic love interest of the main character. As I was watching this documentary, I was captured by a thought ...

It's amazing how impacted our acceptance or rejection of something becomes when we know the whole story.

Everyone loves a good love story. Everyone loves a good redemption story. *Pretty Woman* is both, wrapped up in a two-hour, feel-good, candy-coated shell. It is any wonder the movie ran in theaters for almost a year and ended up smashing box office numbers worldwide? I think, deep down, people found they could relate to Julia Robert's character. Deep down, we all feel broken, used up, and out of bounds. Deep down, we all feel our own need for redemption. If Pretty Woman's got a chance, maybe I do, too.

So what does this have to do with the church? As I look at the story of scripture, I see a story of redemption. I see a groom (Jesus Christ) willing to lay his life down for his bride (the church) (see Ephesians 5:21-33). I see a God who loved the world so much that He sent His son, Jesus Christ, to redeem a world that couldn't redeem itself. From cover to cover, the Bible is a redemption story. That is what I see when I look at the Bible.

And yet that is not what I see when I look at the church in the United States.

All across the landscape of American evangelicalism today, I see the bride of Christ prostituting itself, selling out on so many of the things that make the church the bride of Christ, all to protect the lifestyle we want, the comfort we have become accustomed to and daresay even addicted to, and the relationship we have with a God (as we established in earlier chapters) of our own creation. A God we do not love. Rather, it's just a God we service. It's not faith, it's prostitution. It's not worship, it's idolatry.

I realize I may be actively offending some of you who are reading this right now with the analogy I chose to use in this chapter. All I can say is, "Don't kill the messenger." You see, I didn't come up with this analogy. I borrowed it from Jesus. I took it right out of the pages of scripture. Prostitution is a common theme God uses throughout scripture to paint the picture of His wandering church. So reel those potential judgments back in, hit the pause button on your temptation to "cancel" me at this point, and ask yourself an honest question:

Why did God choose the metaphor of a prostitute?

The simple and short answer is—it's familiar. Too familiar. In fact, sacred prostitution used to be part of a lot of false religions. Though I wouldn't recommend this as your primary source of research on ANY topic, a quick Wikipedia search will show you just how common this idea was:

> *Sacred prostitution, temple prostitution, cult prostitution, and religious prostitution are purported rites consisting of paid intercourse performed in the context of religious worship, possibly as a form of fertility rite or divine marriage (hieros gamos). Scholars prefer the terms "sacred sex" or "sacred sexual rites" in cases where payment for services is not involved.*

While sacred prostitution was not a part of worship of God, the Israelites had a nasty habit of getting caught up in syncretism or the blending of the worship of false gods of other nations with their worship of the one true God. Throughout the pages of scripture, there are warnings about the danger of sliding into these practices and allowing pure worship of the one true God to become diluted and watered down.

For instance, in Leviticus 19, in a section of the law dedicated to teaching the Israelites about holiness in their personal conduct, we find warning about allowing our daughters to become caught up in the practice of prostitution. And in Deuteronomy 23, there is a warning specifically about not only participating in temple prostitution but even about tithing off the money earned in temple prostitution:

> 17 "*No Israelite, whether man or woman, may become a*

temple prostitute. [18] *When you are bringing an offering to fulfill a vow, you must not bring to the house of the Lord your God any offering from the earnings of a prostitute, whether a man or a woman, for both are detestable to the Lord your God.* (Deuteronomy 23:17-18 NLT)

I know what you're thinking—that's the Old Testament! That's so outdated! After all, Jesus came to free us from the law! Right?

Wrong.

Jesus didn't come to free us from the law. He came to fulfill the law. While we are no longer prisoners to the legalistic standards of the Pharisees, still the call is not a call to allow the grace of Jesus to becomc our excuse to sin. That would be akin to marrying someone we don't love just because they're rich and can provide us a comfortable life. That's not love. That's gold-digging.

And yet, this metaphor spans the pages of scripture. In 1 Corinthians 6, we see Paul's appeal that our bodies are one with Christ and warning against uniting Christ's body with a prostitute. It's a picture of how when we are doing the darkest things, things we think are hidden and unseen, Christ is there with us. Anyone else just get super convicted? I know I did.

Even in the final pages of God's word, we find in Revelation 17 a reference to Babylon, "Great Prostitute." Even at the end of the book, humanity is still guilty of uniting ourselves with a prostitute. Revelation talks about how world leaders have committed adultery with this prostitute and how those who have chosen this world over God have become "drunk on the wine of her immorality."

Bottom line, God chose this metaphor because this is what we have been guilty of for a very long time. I actually think there are two primary ways we are guilty of spiritual prostitution:

First, we are guilty of cheating on God with prostitutes.

One of the most famous stories of prostitution in scripture is found in the Old Testament book of Hosea. We can't look at the whole thing together, so I'll summarize for you. God commands Hosea, a faithful man and one of His prophets, to marry a woman who was actively involved in prostitution and who, according to God, will leave Hosea and return to her life of prostitution. Hosea obeys God and marries a prostitute named Gomer, who does exactly what God says she is going to do.

Now, listen. I don't know what hard things you think God has asked you to do, but compared to some of the stuff God asks some of His prophets to do in scripture, we've got it easy! He asked Jeremiah to preach his whole life without anyone listening to him. Ever. He asked Jonah to preach on the streets of a godless city where he was likely to be killed for his message. One of my favorites is when he asks Ezekiel to lie on his side for almost a year cooking his food over human poop. Yup, that's right—poop. When Ezekiel asks for a little mercy in this call, God allows him to use animal poop instead of human poop. Gee, thanks, God.

My point is, God asks these prophets to do some pretty bizarre things, just to make His point. And Hosea is no exception to that rule. God wants to paint a picture of His love for Israel and how, like Gomer, Israel is guilty of prostituting herself—of being unfaithful to their relationship with God. In one of the most beautiful passages in the Old Testament, God compares His love for unfaithful Israel with Hosea's love for his unfaithful prostitute of a wife:

> *But then I will win her back once again. I will lead her into the desert and speak tenderly to her there.* (Hosea 2:14 NLT)

Now, I don't have any strong scholarly proofs to back up what

I'm about to say here ... but I've always read this promise from God in Hosea, and in my mind, I can't help but think of this as a reference to Jesus on the cross. While all of humanity turned its back, Jesus went to the cross to win us back again. To redeem his bride. Ephesians 5 talks about a washing of the bride of Christ—a work He does for His bride to purify her for Himself—to make her without spot and wrinkle. The cross is this redeeming work.

As I read the words of Hosea 2:14, I see Jesus saying, "I will lead her into the desert and speak tenderly to her there." I see Jesus carrying His cross outside the city to Golgotha, located in the wilderness just outside the city. I see Him in the desert (as it were), being nailed to the cross. And I hear Him speaking tenderly to us there. There could be no more tender words than "Father forgive them ... for they don't know what they are doing."

Could it be through Hosea's marriage to Gomer, God was not only showing His great love for His people but also pointing to the cross? Could it be He was not only comparing Himself to a husband whose wife has committed adultery but also pointing to the way He would redeem His bride?

I get it. The temptation right now is to take a "that was then, this is now" approach to this conversation. Sure, you can point to Israel's struggle in this area. This metaphor of prostitution and being unfaithful is really a metaphor pointing to idolatry, right? We don't have idols anymore ... do we? As it turns out, while our idols don't sit enshrined in our homes where we bow down to them ... perhaps they are, and perhaps we do. When things in our lives hold more value or merit more attention than God does, that is, by its very definition, idolatry. It's unfaithfulness. In an article in *Lima News* titled "Spiritual Prostitution in the Church," author Sharon Jefferson says as much:

> *The children of Israel were accused of having many lovers, and today the Lord is saying the very same thing about the*

church ... I am wondering what would happen if the Lord were to ask a preacher today to marry a prostitute as He asked Hosea. What would the reaction be? I can just imagine. God was making an example to Israel of all of their backslidings. He was speaking of the coming judgment, a warning, so the people would repent and return to Him. Nothing has changed today. The Lord is calling His church back to Him. We must remember that anything we put before the Lord as preventing Him from being first in our life has become an idol before God.

Today, I think the evangelical church is filled with Gomers. I think everywhere you look, you see those who have united themselves with Jesus, and yet we are guilty of unfaithfulness. We are guilty of going back to an old life we can't let go of. We are guilty of a duplicitous relationship with God—where He is not our one and only. We are guilty of moments of unfaithfulness. Pockets of sin. We're guilty of pretending we are all in on this relationship but hiding things in the dark. We are guilty of worshiping other gods—though, today, these gods don't look like statues or idols. Still, idolatry runs through our veins. We worship idols like success, status, money, power, appearance, and social standing. We claim they are not idols. We claim we aren't being unfaithful. But let me ask you a question about faithfulness.

When am I guilty of being unfaithful to my wife? Is it when I physically cheat on her with someone else? Or is it when I make someone or something else of greater value in my heart? Those who answer in the former are already guilty of the latter. Those who say, "It's not unfaithfulness until you actually cross the line," have already crossed lines. If you have to justify your behavior, you're already in the wrong. Right doesn't need to be justified.

This is where I think a lot of the evangelical church is in their relationship with Jesus. We are justifying. While we may not be guilty of "cheating" outright on God, we are consistently guilty of making other things of greater value in our lives than our relationship with Jesus. We go to church. We say we love God. But we're having emotional affairs left and right. We are Gomers.

As it turns out, this is the more obvious form of unfaithfulness. But I mentioned, I think there are TWO ways we are guilty of spiritual prostitution. There is another way we are guilty of spiritual unfaithfulness:

Second, we are guilty of making the church a prostitute.

Let's go back to *Pretty Woman* for a moment. One of the key elements of this movie is that Julia Roberts' character won't kiss on the lips. According to her, there is nothing more intimate than kissing. Sex is sex. But kissing is different. Kissing is intimate. For a prostitute, sex is transactional. There is no intimacy involved in it. This is how you know in the movie that the two main characters are in love. For the first time, they kiss. And when they do, everything is different.

I rather like that picture of intimacy. As we established early on in this journey, sex can be intimate, but intimacy is much more than just sex. It's being fully known. In God's holy and beautiful pursuit of us, He is after intimacy. He is not a God who is sitting back, aloof and uninterested in us. In actuality, God is pursuing us. He is described as the "Hound of Heaven" by Francis Thompson in his 1890 poem. He is the God who SO loved us, He sent His son, Jesus, to redeem us. He is a God who sent Christ to die for us while we were still sinners. He is the father of the prodigal son, throwing off all restraint and dignity, running to us and embracing and even kissing us. God is after intimacy.

And so are we, we claim. And yet our actions betray us. If someone is after intimacy and you offer them less than the real thing, it will be blindingly obvious. And it is blindingly obvious that while ALL Christians claim to long for an intimate relationship with God, MOST of them approach God not relationally but transactionally. We are all guilty of regularly taking the greatest love the world has ever known and making it transactional. Faith, for so many, has become about what God can DO for us and what we get out of the relationship. Everything from church attendance to serving to tithing—it's all about balancing or even hoping to tip the scales in our favor. We seek God, but only on Sunday. The rest of the week, it's anyone's guess where our passions will take us.

COVID-19 revealed this in a massive way across the United States, as church attendance took a massive hit. So many pointed to a lack of relevance in the church. And yet, the gospel of Jesus Christ doesn't become irrelevant—ever. Certainly, churches are guilty of failing to present the gospel well, but at the end of the day, the truth of Jesus Christ is unchanging. What changed was the value the average attender saw in being at church. When given the opportunity to not be there, most "Christians" did a simple ROI (return on investment) inventory. They weighed the value of being at church with what they gained by not being there. Once the price of attendance became too high and the value (in their minds) to being part of church became too low, they moved on.

Yeah, that sounds like intimacy to me.

Please hear me. I am not claiming that church attendance and love for Christ are the same thing—far from it. You can and should have a very real and personal relationship with your heavenly Father that is not dependent on the church. And yet one sort of highlights the other. Going to church doesn't mean you have an intimate relationship with God. Going to church is sort of like date night. Going on a regular date night with your spouse doesn't mean you have a high level of intimacy. And yet those who have a high level of intimacy don't regularly skip date night. They WANT that focused time on their relationship. They crave it. When we approach our faith transactionally, it's all about checks and balances. It's about doing what's required. Intimacy isn't about what's required. Intimacy is insatiable. It can never get enough. It hungers and thirsts for more. This is a picture of kingdom intimacy.

Do you want to be intimate with God?

In 2005, Jesus Culture wrote a song that took the church by storm titled "How He Loves." And yet, though it was incredibly popular among churches, most churches were guilty of making a lyrical change before introducing it to their congregations. They claimed the change was due to "theological issues" they had with the original lyrics. I think the real problem was simpler than that. I think when Kim Walker would sing the lyrics in question, her intimacy with God would ooze out everywhere, and the combination of that intimacy and of some very intimate lyrics made most evangelicals uncomfortable.

If you sang this in your local church in the 2000s, you may have sung lyrics that told you that heaven meets earth with an "unforeseen kiss." That is how most evangelical churches edited the lyrics to make them more palpable. That is not what Jesus Culture or John Mark McMillan wrote. They described that moment when Jesus' presence invades earth much more intimately:

> So *heaven meets earth like a sloppy wet kiss and my heart turns violently inside of my chest. And I don't have time to maintain these regrets when I think about (The way). That he loves us.*

How does that lyric make you feel? It's intimate. It made a lot of Christians feel uncomfortable. And that's the problem.

I heard once that kissing in Hebrew culture was described as a moment when "two souls touch." Wow. Maybe Julia Roberts was right in *Pretty Woman*. When Jesus came to earth to carry out the redemption of humanity, heaven was kissing the earth .... because God is, without question, seeking intimacy with His people. Heaven met earth with a sloppy, wet kiss.

The question is, does your heart turn violently inside of your chest? When you think about God's love for you, do you find yourself overwhelmed with His love? Do you find yourself leaning away? Or do you find yourself keeping God at arm's length? How the heart of God must break as generation after generation takes the greatest world the love has ever known and turns it into a transactional experience. Is it any wonder He was willing to go to such great lengths to get our attention? And this is something we see God doing over and over again because of His great love for us.

In the garden, He gave Adam and Eve a choice, and they were unfaithful. And yet we still see Him going to great lengths to love them. He made clothes to cover their nakedness—but where did those clothes come from? He sacrificed animals, and there was the shedding of blood in order to cover our shame.

Throughout the Old Testament, we read about God's love for His people Israel, and we also read about their constant failure and unfaithfulness, prostituting themselves with the idols of other nations. We read about a sacrificial system that seems barbaric to us but to them meant redemption. We read about how pure and spotless lambs were sacrificed and their blood was shed to cover or "atone" for the sins of the people. Again and again, Israel would be unfaithful. Again and again, there would be the shedding of blood in order to cover our shame.

In John chapter 6, we read about Jesus miraculously feeding 5,000 men, plus women and children, using a small boy's sack lunch of bread and fish. Jesus miraculously multiplies the loaves so there is enough for everyone. The next day, it says the people came looking for more bread. Instead, Jesus offers Himself. In what seems like a bizarre metaphor, Jesus describes Himself as the bread of life. He is the only thing that can truly sustain us eternally. Jesus pushes this metaphor to the limits, stretching the faith of everyone who believes:

> 47 *"I tell you the truth, anyone who believes has eternal*
> *life.* 48 *Yes, I am the bread of life!* 49 *Your ancestors ate manna*
> *in the wilderness, but they all died.* 50 *Anyone who eats the*
> *bread from heaven, however, will never die.* 51 *I am the living*
> *bread that came down from heaven. Anyone who eats this bread will live forever; and this bread, which I will offer so the world may live, is my flesh."* (John 6:47–51 NLT)
>
> Um … excuse me? Could you say that again?
>
> 53 *So Jesus said again, "I tell you the truth, unless you eat the flesh of the Son of Man and drink his blood, you cannot have*
> *eternal life within you.* 54 *But anyone who eats my flesh and*
> *drinks my blood has eternal life, and I will raise that person*
> *at the last day.* 55 *For my flesh is true food, and my blood is*
> *true drink.* (John 6:53–55 NLT)

It's probably no surprise as you keep reading that the people seem confused. This is even a moment where many who had been following walk away. What they don't seem to realize is that this is not only a continuation of a pattern we have seen since creation … it's actually a fulfillment of God's part in the redemption of process. For generations, they have been living under a sacrificial system where over and over again, the blood of animals had to be shed to cover our shame. Now Jesus, the "spotless lamb of God," uses that same metaphor to foreshadow what's to come on the cross. When He speaks of His blood and His flesh, He's referring to how His life will be given and His blood will be shed so that, once and for all, the shedding of blood can cover our shame.

We live with the gift of perspective. We have the scriptures, so we know that after saying these hard to accept words, Jesus would give us the practice of communion as a way of regularly remembering His broken body and shed blood. And yet even with that perspective, we often forget just how much it cost Jesus to cover our shame and nakedness. We forget that without the shedding of blood, there can be no forgiveness. Sometimes we even forget we need forgiveness.

I wonder how many of us said yes to Jesus when we are starving for bread ... but now He's offering Himself, and we're struggling with what that might mean. I wonder how many just want to be fed, but faith actually requires so much more. I wonder how many of us showed up for the miracles but don't like the hard teaching. And so once again, we are wandering. And once again, He is waiting to cover our shame.

Jesus shares this hard teaching in John 6 about how faith is about more than what you get out of it. It's a relationship that requires sacrifice from both parties involved. It's an invitation into more. And sometimes it requires you to have faith when you don't understand and to stay committed even in hard things. And in that moment, many walk away. Jesus turns to the disciples to see what they will do.

> **66** *At this point many of his disciples turned away and deserted him.* **67** *Then Jesus turned to the Twelve and asked, "Are you also going to leave?"* **68** *Simon Peter replied, "Lord, to whom would we go? You have the words that give eternal life.* **69** *We believe, and we know you are the Holy One of God." (John 6:66–69 NLT)*

As well-intentioned as he was in saying this, even Peter would eventually deny Jesus. When push came to shove and Jesus was arrested, tried, and crucified for you and me, His closest disciples scattered, and Peter had denied three times he even knew Jesus. Israel's religious leaders were the ones who called for His crucifixion. The entire world He came to save at best turned their backs on Him as He was saving them and, at worst, were actually responsible for the nails that pierced His flesh.

The bride of Christ had prostituted herself. She had been so unfaithful. And yet, there, in the desert, He spoke lovingly to her. Just as He had Hosea take Gomer back in her worst moment when she was at her lowest—and not just take her back ... but BUY her back ... so Jesus, as He hung on the cross, chose to speak lovingly of us.

"Father, forgive them.
They don't know what they're doing."

But then I will win her back once again. I will lead her into the desert and speak tenderly to her there. (Hosea 2:14 NLT)

CHAPTER 7

Unmet Expectations

Why the greatest problem in any relationship is me.

My dad was an avid storyteller. Now, if you don't know what avid means, I want you to set this book down and Google it right now because it's important that you understand what I AM and what I am NOT saying. Go ahead, look it up ... I'll wait.

• • •

Are we ready? Are we all on the same page? Okay, good. Let me start again. My dad was an avid storyteller. He absolutely **LOVED** to tell stories. He was not necessarily, however, a **GOOD** storyteller. His stories were always either way funnier or way more meaningful to **him** than they were to **me**. Now, I attribute some of that to my age and immaturity—I simply didn't have enough depth and life experience to fully appreciate what my dad had going on. But I still attribute most of it to my dad.

My father was a walking dad joke machine before dad jokes were a thing. And you might think, "Oh, how fun! I love dad jokes!" Guess what? Me, too. I think the power of dry wit, simplistic and well-delivered punch lines, with just a dash of sarcasm, is truly an art form. My dad was no artist.

What I can only assume was one of his top stories (given he told it to me probably 100 times during my child) was a lesson about a sailor with a big curly mustache on a navy ship. My dad was a United States Navy guy, which may have been why he liked this story so much. In the story, there is a sailor known for two things—his extremely sour disposition and his extremely large Curly-Q mustache. Most of the sailors would complain about just how grumpy and sour this particular sailor was.

One day, several of them decided to play a prank on him to sort of teach him a lesson. They waited until he was fast asleep after a long shift, and they covered his mustache with a foul-smelling cheese dip. When the man woke up, he immediately began to complain about the absolutely horrid stench in the room.

"This ROOM stinks!" the man boomed, and he proceeded to storm out into the hallway of the ship.

"This HALLWAY stinks!" the man bellowed loudly as he moved toward the stairs and started climbing to the main deck.

"These STAIRS stink!" the man shouted as he crested the final turn toward the top of the stairwell and burst out onto the main deck. Running to the edge of the ship and taking a deep whiff, the man screamed at the top of his lungs ...

"The WHOLE WORLD stinks!"

This is the point where my dad would start to laugh uncontrollably. For some reason, this story tickled him. It hit him just right, and every time he told it, I had to wait before his howling laughter subsided and he had wiped away his tears of joy before he finally proclaimed the moral of the story. It's hard to believe it, but that moral has survived for forty years in my mind and is now the perfect setup for what I want to talk about in this chapter. Here's the moral of the story:

If you think the whole world stinks,
it just might be you.

I share this story with you partly to garner your sympathy—yes, my whole life with my father was like that! But really, I just think that while his story is (quite literally) "cheesy," it's also true. And it illustrates so well for us this idea of unmet expectations.

In any situation you are in, whether by yourself or with others, you are being driven by a set of expectations. There are often expectations placed on you by others—and certainly that comes into play in any relationship. But what I am referring to right now are the expectations that you have formed in your own mind—sometimes consciously and more often unconsciously—that affect how you see the whole world around you. And one of the biggest problems about expectations is that they aren't uniform. Sure, you can and, in a lot of cases, probably SHOULD have a clearly communicated basic set of expectations for any relationship you enter into. But most of the time, we are living life through the lens of our own self-created, and honestly, self-focused expectations.

Why are all old people mad? (At the time of writing this, I'm forty-five, and yes, I am solidly placing myself in this category.) Because we have expectations. We think a certain way, and we expect everyone around us, particularly the younger generations, to think like we do. After all, it's common sense. But they don't think like we do. And yet that doesn't stop us from expecting them to or from being frustrated over and over when they continue to see things differently.

We expect the waitress, the store clerk, the teller at the bank, our neighbors to all behave in a way that makes sense to us and to meet expectations we have in our minds of what each of those individuals should do. We have roles they play in our lives, and we expect them to know what those roles are and to conform to those roles. And when they don't, it affects our outlook on life. Let's just say I've met more and more people lately who are covered with smelly cheese dip.

This is human nature. Every relationship I enter into, I can only enter into it as me. And I bring my own set of expectations with me. My assumption is that my expectations are correct and that everyone shares that same sense of expectations. Nothing could be further from the truth.

In fact, it's my theory that the greatest contributing factor to friction in human relationships—the thing that actually makes any relationship hard—is navigating the collision between reality and our deeply held unmet expectations.

I want you to think back to the times in your life when relationships have ended poorly. I'm guessing nobody has to think too hard to come up with examples. All of us have relationships that have failed—be it a relationship with a boss or an employee that ended poorly, a friendship that fizzled, a dating relationship that went south, an engagement that ended up "disengaging," or a marriage that ended in divorce. For some, we've even had family relationships—the supposed tightest of bonds—go off the rails.

And at the center of every relationship that has ever ended poorly, what you will find are unmet expectations. In fact, I'll go a step further—every broken relationship that has ever existed has, at its core, been about unmet expectations. I dated WAY too much when I was young (I do NOT recommend it). As I have already stated in earlier chapters, I love LOVE. For me, I knew the risk of any relationship, but in my lovestruck heart, the risk was, in my mind, always worth the reward. And yet without fail, relationship after relationship ended. You would think that I would learn after a certain number of heartbreaks. And yet I just kept going back.

Sometimes, I would be the one ending the relationship. When I did, I'll have you notice it was NEVER because of something I did. We don't end friendships because of how bad of a friend WE have been. We don't end relationships because of expectations WE didn't live up to and all the areas WE fell short. Whenever I "broke up" with a girl, while I might have said, "It's not you, it's me ..." the truth is, it was always them. At least in my mind. I had reached a point where I thought to myself, "This isn't working." And what wasn't working was that the relationship wasn't living up to my what? You guessed it ... **expectations.**

The expectations we bring into any human relationship tend to center around what that relationship is going to feel like for me, what that person is going to do for me, and how I am going to feel when I am in that relationship. While we subconsciously know that relationships take two, people almost never think of their part of the relationship and what entering into that relationship is going to require of themselves. When I ended relationships with these girls, it was always because THEY didn't live up to MY expectations. I was never thinking of ways I may not have lived up to THEIR expectations.

And, believe it or not, more often than not, it wasn't me who was ending the relationship! I was often the one who was "broken up" with. I know! I'm still shocked about it—I mean ... I'm pretty great! What kind of unrealistic expectations did they have of me anyway? In fact, when I would get broken up with, I would almost always ask the girl, "WHY? What did I DO?" I wanted to know what I could have done differently. And while the answers were always fairly generic and vague and gave me no clarity on what I could have done differently, it was clear. I had not lived up to their expectations.

This is the human condition. We live with expectations for every person and every situation. We can't help it. And while we think what we expect of others is more than reasonable, we often feel the expectations others place on us seem extreme. We also tend to view ourselves with a whole lot more grace when it comes to expectations than we naturally offer to others.

For example, in the church, it's common to see people call out a sin in someone else's life while simultaneously justifying sin in their own. When others make mistakes, it's sinful behavior. When I make mistakes, it's a lapse in judgment, a weak moment, or a vulnerable spot. I'm not sinful, just misguided. Obviously God's grace covers me, but that other guy—I'm not so sure.

Jesus often addressed this in his teaching, encouraging us, as we see in the golden rule, to "do unto others as you would have them do unto you." In fact, in Matthew 7, Jesus goes as far as to point out our tendency to have unfair and unrealistic expectations of one another and to focus on the faults of others while ignoring our own:

> [1] "*Do not judge others, and you will not be judged.* [2] *For you will be treated as you treat others. The standard you use in judging is the standard by which you will be judged.*
>
> [3] "*And why worry about a speck in your friend's eye when you have a log in your own?* [4] *How can you think of saying to your friend, 'Let me help you get rid of that speck in your eye,' when you can't see past the log in your own eye?* [5] *Hypocrite! First get rid of the log in your own eye; then you will*

see well enough to deal with the speck in your friend's eye. (Matthew 7:1-5 NLT)

Jesus describes ignoring a LOG in our own eye while pointing out a SPECK in our friend's eye. Some friend. It's so easy to be blind to the inequity between the exceptions we hold others to vs. the expectations we have for ourselves.

• • •

At this point, it should probably go without saying that if this is our reality with one another, it may be having a significant impact on how we navigate our relationship with God. Remember, every one of us brings expectations to every relationship. Whether you grew up in church or you have never darkened the doors of one, you have expectations of God and what He is like. Those of us who believe in God, we bring a whole set of expectations with us into the relationship. We'll unpack that more here in a bit.

For those who question if there really is a God or who flat-out deny God, this lack of faith usually hovers around some set of unmet expectations. We have expectations for a God we don't even know if we believe in. We just belief that IF God existed, He would be a certain way. IF God existed, He would obviously meet my expectations of what a God should be. For those who don't believe, those expectations tend to surround the nature of God. What is God like? How does He behave? I can't tell you how many people I have met in my life who don't believe in God and yet are angry at Him at the same time because of their unmet expectations.

If God exists, then there wouldn't be so much evil in the world! If God were real, He would never let this happen to me! If God is so good, then why doesn't He stop all the bad people? Even those who don't believe in God have a host of unmet expectations surrounding how the God they don't believe in has failed them.

Those of us who do claim to believe typically can expect at some point on our faith journey to have a crisis of that belief. And that crisis is almost always brought on by God behaving in a way in this relationship that does not match up with the expectations we have brought into it. This is something I think would be healthy for every believer to acknowledge—you have brought unrealistic expectations into this relationship with your creator. Somewhere along the way, you have told yourself things about God that are not true. You have made yourselves promises on behalf of God that He never made. You have viewed God's role in your life as something more or less than it is or was ever meant to be. At some point in your faith journey, you will have a crisis of faith that ultimately comes down to some version of "God, I thought you were ___________, but you're not." And the problem will never be with Him. It will always be with you.

God didn't fail you. God didn't change. God didn't go back on His word. He may have gone back on the promise you made yourself and then put into His mouth. But He did not fail to keep His actual promises to you. When it comes to His nature and His promises, God is absolutely and sometimes annoyingly consistent. And yet most Christians at some point find themselves mad at God, doubting God, wondering if God is actually good ... or if He is even actually there. And the core of your anger has to do with false expectations that you brought into this relationship.

When you read the New Testament, most of the frustration people had with Jesus had to do with unmet expectations. The Israelites thought He would deliver them from the Romans. The Pharisees were so set in their expectations of the Messiah that they would overlook miracles because they didn't think the Messiah would break their rules. He couldn't be God because He didn't meet their expectations. So set were the people in their expectations that eventually they had no choice but to kill Him. Jesus was crucified on a cross built out of unmet expectations.

OK, so let's get real, shall we? This isn't some intellectual spewing platitudes. This isn't some pastor just telling you what you should believe. While I AM a pastor, I'd likely barely qualify as an intellectual ... and I'm not speaking to you right now as one either. This is a real person speaking from real life experience. I AM what I'm talking about. I'm describing myself. Or at least who I WAS. My story is just like yours. I'm a person who entered into this relationship with Jesus with certain expectations—and who had to wrestle with the reality of my faith when He didn't live up to them. I'm going to tell you that story in a minute. But first, let me tell you the story of another person. A regular guy who loved God. His name was Job.

I'm not going to do a whole study on the life of Job. While I will always encourage you to read God's word, I'm not even necessarily recommending that you go read the whole story of Job. But it is a case study in unmet expectations. It starts with God holding a court of some sort. "The Satan" approaches God, and God begins to celebrate this man named Job and his obedience. Satan claims that of course Job is faithful—God meets all his expectations. But if things didn't go Job's way ... that would change things.

As Christians, we don't like to read about what happens next because, if we're honest, a God who would allow Satan to test Job the way He does doesn't fit with our ... ahem ... expectations. God gives Satan permission to test Job, and by the time things are done, the only thing Job HASN'T lost is his actual life, three not-so-great friends, and a peach of a wife who tells him to curse God and die.

The three friends are trying to be helpful. Their only problem is that they also bring their false expectations about God to the party. God rewards the righteous and punishes the wicked. That is who He is. That is how He is. Job is being punished—therefore he must be guilty of some serious wickedness. Job claims he hasn't done anything (and he is telling the truth!). But the expectations his friends have brought to the table about God make it impossible for them to believe Him. They cannot (or will not) believe in a God who would allow Job to go through this.

Job himself is left wrestling with his own expectations. He KNOWS God is faithful. He KNOWS he hasn't done anything to merit this punishment. And yet there he is, sitting in dust and ashes, scraping his sores with broken pottery, being blamed by his friends, cursed by his wife, and feeling completely abandoned by a God he thought he understood. Finally, it all becomes too much, and Job's anger with God overflows. For several chapters, Job lets God have it with both barrels. The weight of his unmet expectations finally becomes more than he can bear, and he lets God know just how he is feeling.

Finally, God gets a turn to defend Himself. But the strange thing is ... he doesn't. Instead, he gives Job sort of a tour of the universe. He describes to Job the vastness of all He has created. He points him to the beauty of some of the creatures He has made, being intentional to point to two creatures—Behemoth and Leviathan (Job 40-41 in the Bible)—who are both beautiful and also completely terrifying. It's as if God is reminding Job that God Himself is often both beautiful and also terrifying.

In a way, it's as if God is confronting Job's unmet expectations. It's as if God is challenging whether Job really ever knew Him at all. It's like God is saying, "Job, look at the world around you. I made it all. **How could you look at the world around you in all its complexity and still have a view of me that's so simple?** In a universe that's so big, how can your expectations of me be so very small?"

Now, in no way am I claiming that Job's story is my own. I

have, in the words of Third Eye Blind, lived a "semi-charmed" kind of life. I'm aware every day of the blessings I have received in this life and in some cases have always known. I was adopted into a Christian home. It was FAR from perfect, but it was in large part the reason I was introduced to this faith that has come to define so much of my life. I've known a ton of hardship in this life, but I've also been given a ton of opportunity. I followed God's call on my life, and at times, it has been the toughest thing I've ever known. But it also put me on a path where I met my wife, the love of my life and my better half for sure. I'm happily married for (at the time of this writing) twenty-two years. I have three amazing kids who love God, love us, and are seeking to discover His plan for their lives. I get to lead a pretty amazing church—a church my wife and I got to plant together with some dear friends—friends who then went on to plant their own church. I could spend pages listing the blessings I have known. I could also spend pages listing the tragedies and hardships. They are a mixed bag in this thing called life.

My point in all of this is that I'm not unaware of my blessings. Again, I haven't suffered anything like Job suffered. But what I have in common with him (and I'm guessing you might, too) is that when life happens and the blessed life becomes a little (or in some cases a lot) more bumpy, we find ourselves in a place of questioning.

One of the things I have always admired about Job is that even in the midst of his loss, his hurt, his anger, and his questioning, he never turns his back on God. He yells at God. He tells God how He is really feeling. He questions a LOT of things. But he never quits on God.

That's where I found myself in 2020. Maybe you did, too. We moved to Sioux Falls (my hometown) in 2008 and planted Ransom Church in 2009. From the get-go, we saw God's hand of blessing all over the church. My family was a different story. Over the next ten years, we would walk through the declining health of my father as the multiple sclerosis he had dealt with my whole life finally started winning the battle. I would walk through bank fraud against my parents, the constant hospitalization of my father, the onset of Alzheimer's disease and dementia in my mother, and the cleaning out, updating, and sale of their home (a home my dad built that I grew up in). I would walk through the sale of several rental properties and my mom's business. I would put my mom in a memory care unit of a nursing home. I would spend years caring for my parents, watching my dad waste away physically and my mom waste away mentally. In 2014, I would bury my dad. In 2019, I would bury my mom. After ten years, I was weary. It was hard to believe that season was over. But God had continued to bless on the church front the entire time. I remember thinking during the Christmas season of 2019, "I think we are turning a corner."

Then the world lost its mind.

2020 turned the whole world upside down. Everyone reading this who lived through it was directly affected. Everyone knows someone who died. Everyone has some level of PTSD from masks and home confinement. And the worst part—everyone chose a side. And the world fractured. And for those in the evangelical church world, we watched church as we know it fracture as well.

**Ransom Church didn't just fracture. It broke.
It came apart at the seams.**

I went into the pandemic confident that despite all the things we didn't know, I knew our church was strong enough to weather this storm and the trust we had was high enough that people would stick through us as we muddled our way through making impossible decision after impossible decision. By the end of 2021, I found myself gutted. I felt like I was sitting in the ashes of something we had given over a decade of our life to building. Over half our church was gone. We had three campuses in Sioux Falls but could easily fit into one. We were financially shell-shocked. We were forced like so many to do layoffs. But none of this was what hurt the most. What hurt the most was the friendly fire.

Now, I mentioned earlier that I'm not naive here. I'm in no way comparing myself to what Job suffered. But what I definitely found myself able to do was relate to Job ... particularly when it came to the "encouragement" of his so-called friends. Every Christian on the planet was dealing with unmet expectations due to this global pandemic. They were mad at God, and I was lucky enough in so many cases to be the one they held responsible. People in our church would tell me they were leaving and would cite some unmet expectations they had of God that they were holding Ransom Church, and myself in particular, responsible for. I would have people from the congregation who were mad at me about a decision tell me how evil I was for making the decision I had made. I remember one time where in the same day, I received two different emails from two different families, both raking me over the coals about the same decision—and both on OPPOSITE sides of the decision. One called me a coward for not taking a stronger stance. One called me a liberal dictator for taking as strong a stance as I did. Both left the church.

I did that ... times a thousand. Or more. Honestly, I lost count. I remember thinking—"this is how Job must have felt being hammered by friends who were telling him it was his fault these things had happened." These well-meaning individuals sat next to Job during his season of greatest suffering and blamed him for their unmet expectations. Like Job, I found myself having some very real conversations with God in that season. But I also found myself unable to "curse God and die." I found that as bad as things were, I knew enough about God to know He was good. And though I couldn't understand why He allowed some of the things He did, I never lost hope in who I knew He was. People—now I definitely lost hope in people. I lost hope in the church. But I never lost hope in God. I yelled at Him. I challenged Him to explain Himself. But I never lost hope in Him.

Finally, God spoke. And when he did, like Job, He felt no need to explain Himself to me. Instead, He had me take a deep look at who I was. And in a season of deep introspection, I came to realize all the expectations I had brought into this relationship that I had obligated God to but that He had never promised. I had assumed that as long as I was faithful, I would always experience this same kind of blessing. I had allowed my identity to be caught up in the "success" of the church. And when all that perceived success fell apart like a house of cards, I lost myself. I lost my way. I went through a very dark place, and when I emerged on the other side, I found out a truth about myself. And it's something I think is true for all of us:

The greatest problem in any relationship is me.

Yes, lots of people had done lots of hurtful things. But I was the one who took them all personally. Yes, the church had gotten a lot smaller. But I was the one who let my value get tied up in the size of the church. Yes, I was angry about what had happened. But all of my anger was ultimately a result of my unmet expectations. I found myself in a season of repentance. I found myself in a place with God where, like Job, I could claim, "I thought I knew you. But know I've seen you. And I repent in dust and ashes."

Since that season, God has redefined success for me. I stopped chasing the success of metrics and started chasing the success of obedience. My only goal every day is to lay my head on my pillow and to know I was obedient. Even the writing of this book is an act of obedience—I couldn't say no to him any longer. When obedience to Him is the only thing you're chasing, you can have the "best" day, but you don't take the credit for that day, you simply ask—"was I obedient?" And when you have a terrible day and people tear you apart or you experience a loss or a setback, you don't have to pretend the day was good, but as you lay your head on your pillow, you can ask—"was I obedient?" If the answer to that question is yes, then regardless of what the day turned out to be, your heart is good.

I don't know where you are with God. I don't know if you believe in Him or not. I don't know if life is all roses for you right now or if you find yourself in a crisis of faith. But I do know this like it's a fact. Most of the frustration people have with God and most of the reasons people have for doubting God come down to unrealistic expectations. What expectations do you have about God, and where did they come from? The best way to begin to know what you can truly expect from God is to learn about Him in His word. Nothing will challenge and right-size your faulty expectations of God like reading the Bible. Knowing God's word is critical to knowing God, and it also helps us know His expectations of us in this relationship. We're going to dive into that more in the next chapter. If you find yourself struggling in your faith, I want to challenge you to consider if the problem may not be God.

If the whole world stinks, it might just be you.

CHAPTER 8

D.T.R.

Putting a label on this thing called faith.

It's been a while since we left little second-grade Phill as he savored his dating victory. When we left "mini me" there in the mid-1980s, I had just passed my very first "Will you go out with me" note.

"Will you be my girlfriend?"

Yes No (Circle one)

When I received that note back from my beautiful now-girlfriend, I remember savoring the reality of this newly minted relationship. I had a girlfriend. My very first girlfriend. Now, if you asked me what changed as a result of entering into this legally binding relational agreement with my new "bae" to be her new "beau," I would have to say .... nothing. Over the next few days,

I would feel the sum total of zero difference in our relationship. Actually, not zero. I did get to hold her hand ... twice. #BOOM.

The truth was, we had already been friends. We had already given evidence we really liked each other. We played together at recess and sat together at lunch. There were no cell phones, and social media didn't exist. Neither of us were allowed to use the phone regularly, much less use it to call a "significant other." I didn't even dare to tell my mom I HAD a significant other. We didn't go on dates. I didn't buy her gifts. The only thing that changed was our status among the other second graders. We were together. We were a couple. She was my girlfriend. I was her boyfriend.

We dated for three weeks.

In all honesty, I don't actually remember breaking up. I think we did? If not, then I've been dating the same girl for over forty years, and I have a lot of explaining to do to my wife. Either the breakup had so little impact that I don't remember it, or more likely, the relationship just kind of fizzled. Either way, I was far from the only kid in second grade with a girlfriend. Something in us was drawn to that label, regardless of the vapid nature of the relationship behind it. Needless to say, we never had the DTR.

Now, in case you're not familiar with this classic acronym, DTR stands for "Define the Relationship." In every relationship, while we often put labels on the relationship, we rarely actually define what those labels mean. Now, without question, we're having those conversations in our own heads with ourselves. And we're ASSUMING because we are defining this relationship a certain way that the person we are in the relationship with is defining the relationship the exact same way. Rarely is that actually the case. And so you hear phrases when there is conflict in any relationship that are indicators that the two people in the relationship aren't necessarily on the same page. You'll hear phrases like "I thought we were friends" or "I thought you loved me" and "I thought I meant more to you than that." And while these are often unfair modifiers, they are expressing the dissonance one individual is feeling in the relationship. And when we are talking about dating, ultimately, these all boil down to a couple not being on the same page about their relationship.

Given we just came through an entire chapter on unmet expectations, it should be easy to see how important it is to address your expectations and to truly define whatever relationship you enter into. Rarely does this happen. Lots of expectations with no DTR conversations = lots of unmet expectations = lots of hurt and heartache, tons of breakups, and a country with a 50%+ divorce rate. Most relationship struggles you see come down to couples who are defining the relationship differently. I was watching a movie once and Dave Chappelle was one of the supporting cast. I can't remember the movie, the plot, the cast—nothing. Clearly it was a memorable film. But one thing I remember CLEARLY is a line Dave Chappelle had about relationships and taking relationships to the "next level."

Chappelle's character talked about how in dating relationships, you have to be aware of when it's time to take the relationship to the next level. He said, "I just keep taking it to the next level and the next level after that until eventually ... I have no other choice but to break up with her!"

While this is humorous, it's also heartbreaking. What his character was saying was that in every relationship, he wants to get everything he can out of the relationship until it gets too real for him and then he is going to bail. What a sad commentary on human relationships.

As a romantic at heart who dated way too much, I ran into the opposite problem. I always brought all of my heart to every relationship. It was my goal to treat every girl I ever dated better than anyone had treated her in a relationship before. This was my default setting regardless of how serious I was taking the relationship. As you can imagine, this led to some broken hearts. The problem is that as these girlfriends would experience care, compassion, and sensitivity they were not accustomed to, they would fall ... hard. Way quicker than they should have, they were using phrases like "forever" and "our future together" and talking about how they would "say yes" if I asked. They were defining the relationship one way in their hearts and minds based on how I was treating them. And while I really liked some of these girls, I was not nearly in the same place as quickly as they were. They were forming expectations for the future based on how I was treating them in the present. I actually ended up hurting quite a few girls who were convinced I was "the one." One of them even said when we broke up that I "loved too good to just be a boyfriend." They had all defined this relationship one way in their heads. I had a completely different view of that same relationship. And the dissonance between those views led to turmoil.

When I got to college, I realized that everyone was brining deeper expectations to the idea of relationships. While this may no longer be the case, when I went to college, it seemed like girls weren't interested anymore in dating just to date. They weren't interested in wasting their time on a relationship that was going nowhere and didn't mean anything. They were, in a way, defining the relationship. They wanted to at least have a sense that their relationship with someone had a chance of truly becoming something. And once a couple was dating, the assumption was they were moving toward marriage. This is (I tell myself) why I struggled when I met Steph.

I made myself out earlier in the book to be this bold hero in our relationship ... taking back the ring of the girl I wasn't supposed to be with and buying the ring on the spot for my true love. And all of this is true. But it's not the whole story.

It was obvious to everyone when Steph and I met that there was something there. Everyone, that is, but me. I think deep down I knew, and that scared me. It wasn't Steph's fault. It was all me. I was scared because this relationship felt different. It felt like MORE. I dragged my feet for a long time, until eventually Steph forced us to have the DTR conversation. She asked me point-blank what this relationship was. She was honest with me about how she felt. I actually told her I felt the same way. But I wouldn't commit to the relationship. My mouth was proclaiming something that I wasn't backing up with my actions. Eventually, Steph had had enough, and she let me know it. Again, she defined the relationship for me ... she wanted MORE. And she deserved it.

That's when I did some soul-searching. Define the relationship conversations are really all about counting the cost. Am I invested enough in this relationship that I'm willing to count the cost of staying faithful to it? What is this relationship really? And where is it going? What are my expectations of you in this relationship, and what are your expectations of me in this relationship? In second grade, I just wanted to say I had a girlfriend. And she wanted a boyfriend. And that was enough. At least for a few weeks. But with Steph, it was different. For the first time, I was asking myself the right questions. I was asking myself if I loved her. Was I willing to choose her and to keep choosing her? When this got difficult, was I willing to fight for this relationship? Did it matter that much to me? Was this what God had for me? Was this part of His plan?

This is what it takes to define the relationship. **What you're really defining isn't the relationship. It's the commitment.**

When I finally took the time to feel what I was feeling, to ask the hard questions, and to talk to the Lord about this relationship with Steph, a peace came over me, and I knew. I knew she was the one. I knew I was all in. I knew I was willing to count the cost. Sure, I bought a ring two months into our relationship. But I could have actually proposed that very first day—because I knew. I took Steph to a park that day, sat her down by a pond on a bench, and asked her to be my girlfriend.

She said no.

Truthfully, I had that coming. If I were her, I would have doubted my sincerity, too. But I knew my heart. And I had God's peace. Unfazed, I told her that was fine, and I told her that I was going to keep asking her every day until the day she said yes. Five minutes later ... she did. And we have been together ever since. These many years together have been amazing, but they've also been tumultuous. Our relationship has been tested with so many ups and downs. But my commitment remains ... because I knew what I was getting into. I defined the relationship. I counted the cost. I'm all in.

The reason I think over half the marriages in our country end is because while marriage is designed by God to be the ultimate DTR, most people never take that into account. We spend months planning for the wedding and almost no time planning for the marriage. We stand before friends and family and make promises to love and to cherish through all the ups and downs of life. Richer or poorer. Sickness and health. Good times and bad. Until death parts us. We look each other in the eye and say those things with a straight face, but when those promises are tested, too often we say, "Well, I didn't know it meant THIS." We never had the DTR. We didn't really count the cost. And when forced to, a lot of people just decide the cost is too high. Perhaps that's why we struggle so much when it comes to staying committed to God.

• • •

Did you know it was God who chose to use marriage as a metaphor for his relationship with his church? Human relationships were always meant to reflect divine relationships. Marriage wasn't something God saw and thought, "Hey, that's cool! I think I want my relationship with my church to be like that!" Quite the opposite. God gave us the gift of marriage as a metaphor and a picture of the love He already has for us. Our marriages are meant to be both a reflection and a symbol to the world of God's love for His church, as well as a template for what a covenant relationship is supposed to look like. We're going to dive into that much deeper in our final chapter. For now, I want to look at perhaps the most famous verse on marriage in the Bible to give us some context for just how God outlines and defines a relationship with Him.

Earlier, we talked about the picture of marriage from Ephesians chapter 5. While we often culturally buck at the idea of submission to one another, this passage is nothing if not a powerful DTR conversation. And while we tend to get caught up in the conversation surrounding the expectations of both the husband and wife, we often miss a couple of key DTR moments in this passage. The first is found in Ephesians 5:21:

> *And further, submit to one another out of reverence for Christ. (Ephesians 5:21 NLT)*

Submit ... to one another ...

I wonder how different the world would be if people simply took that piece of advice straight to the relational bank. The picture God paints in the marriage metaphor is not a picture of a one-sided relationship. It's a relationship based on the mutual voluntary submission we talked about in Chapter 4. If this relational picture is meant to serve as a template of our relationship with God, then it's worth noting that the relationship God wants with you isn't one-sided either. It's a relationship where you submit to one another. In marriage, the driving factor behind this mutual voluntary submission is our reverence for Christ. When we submit ourselves to God out of reverence for who He is, we are able to do so knowing He is equally committed to us.

The second key DTR moment found in Ephesians 5 is found in verses 31-32:

> [31] *As the Scriptures say, "A man leaves his father and mother and is joined to his wife, and the two are united into one."* [32] *This is a great mystery, but it is an illustration of the way Christ and the church are one.* (Ephesians 5:31-32 NLT)

Once again, we find Paul making a comparison. A man leaves his father and mother and is joined to his wife, and the two become one. Here Paul is just quoting a well-known creation passage in Genesis:

> [23] *"At last!" the man exclaimed. "This one is bone from my bone, and flesh from my flesh! She will be called 'woman,' because she was taken from 'man.'"* [24] *This explains why a man leaves his father and mother and is joined to his wife, and the two are united into one.* (Genesis 2:23-24 NLT)

In this picture, we have some elements I think are CRITICAL for us to notice. God creates a woman from one of Adam's ribs and brings her to Adam. As the classic dad joke states, Adam took one look at Eve and said, "Woah-man!" And that's where the name woman came from.

Not really. To understand what was happening when Adam called Eve woman, you have to go back to the original Hebrew. I am not a Hebrew Scholar. I'm barely a Hebrew novice. But it doesn't take a scholar to see what is happening in this passage.

The Hebrew word for woman is *'iššâ*.

The Hebrew word for man is *'îš*.

Adam was saying—she will be called *'iššâ* because she was

taken from 'îš. She is named from me because she is LIKE me but is not me ... and ME LIKEY. (Note: This is a loose interpretation of the Hebrew—again, barely a novice here).

The point is this. Adam was recognizing in the creation of Eve that finally there was someone who was like him ... his complement ... his partner. Their relationship was defined by their likeness and by their complement. They were more complete together than they were apart. His proclamation of joy, "At Last!" expresses an internal desire and longing to experience a fuller expression of covenantal relationship. And Genesis says, this covenantal expression explains why a man would leave his father and mother and unite himself to a wife in a clearly defined relationship.

And according to Paul, this is an illustration of the way Christ and the church are one. In fact, if you peek back at the creation story one more time, you see that from the moment of creation, before God even made Adam and Eve, the discussion between Father, son, and Spirit was itself a DTR conversation.

> 26 *Then God said, "Let us make human beings in our image, to be like us. They will reign over the fish in the sea, the birds in the sky, the livestock, all the wild animals on the earth, and the small animals that scurry along the ground.* 27 *So God created human beings in his own image. In the image of God he created them; male and female he created them. (Genesis 1:26-27 NLT)*

God created humanity in His image. He created someone who was like Him ... His complement. He empowered us to have dominion over the earth in our submission to Him. He made us partners in His care of creation. Man was more than just a moment of creative expression. Humanity was an opportunity for relationship. He gave us the ability to love and the ability to choose. He had an internal desire to experience a covenantal relationship with humanity. And when He had created us, He looked over us and saw that it was very good.

Paul is saying to us—when we look all the way back to Adam and Eve and the establishment of human relationships, what we are seeing is a reflection of the divine relationship. God created man and woman to marry, to become one flesh, and to be unified and defined in their relationship by this oneness. But the human covenant we make to one another when a couple is married—it's nothing more than a reflection of the relationship He wants to have with His church.

Across the pages of scripture, you will find a God who again and again offers himself to His people. You will see multiple attempts on God's part to have the DTR with His people. And over and over, you will see people who struggle to submit themselves to those relational expectations. From the Israelites in the Old Testament to the Pharisees and the crowds in the New Testament, you see a God who continues to try to clearly define what it means to follow Him. And the one thing humanity has been consistent on over thousands of years is our inability to live up to our part of the bargain.

Most Christians claim we are "all in" on this relationship. We stand before God and make promises to love and to cherish Him through all the ups and downs of life. For richer or poorer. In sickness and in health. In good times and bad. Believing death can never part us. We look God in the eye and say those things with a straight face, but when those promises are tested, too often we say, "Well, I didn't know it meant THIS." We claim we never had the DTR. Except that we did. Over and over. Or at least He did. God has never stuttered. He has never shifted. His word is clear. He has continued to offer all of Himself. And He has been clear what He expects in return. He expects a relationship. He is giving all of Himself. And He expects all of us in return.

CHAPTER 9

Covenant v. Contract

Reading the fine print on our relationship with Jesus.

This story ends where it started. Back at the box. It's hard for me to admit just how pivotal those choices I made in elementary school were and how they have continued to ripple through every aspect of who I am. I hate to admit that this thing I opened myself up to the very first time I cracked the cover of one of those magazines would be something I would battle for the rest of my life. That's the nature of spiritual strongholds.

Even at that early age, I knew what I was doing was wrong. I knew those images weren't real. I knew what I shared with these women wasn't a relationship ... it was an addiction. I knew that every time I gave in, I was breaking the heart of God. And yet their "siren song" called out to me. At first, I could only hear them calling when I was in that house ... the house with the box. But over time, their voices grew louder. Soon, I could hear them calling even when I lay in my bed at home. I began to feel their pull more and more often, until this temptation became less of a periodic feeling and more like the skin I was living in. To be awake was to be tempted. And try as I may to "plug my ears," I could always hear them calling.

Now, at no point did I turn my back on God. At no point would I have said, "I'm not a Christian anymore." I was still learning about God, growing in my faith, seeking to know Him more. At least most of the time. But there was this growing space in my life that I convinced myself was hidden from everyone. I knew logically this wasn't true. God is everywhere and He sees everything. But when temptation is in the driver's seat, sometimes you just end up going wherever he drives you and justifying it later.

My life became duplicitous. Little by little, I was divided in nature. And I knew it. Remember? Junior Bible Quiz master? I was aware of what the Bible said about this type of behavior. I was aware of verses like Proverbs 11:3:

> *The integrity of the upright guides them, but the unfaithful are destroyed by their duplicity. (Proverbs 11:3 NIV)*

Reading that scripture now, my heart breaks inside me as I see the word duplicity connected to the word unfaithful. I knew in my heart I was being duplicitous. But I had convinced myself I could live the way I was living and still be considered faithful. How foolish. More and more in my life, I was learning that lesson we talked about at the beginning of our journey—**this wasn't just about lust ... it was about control.** I actually think most of the people who call themselves Christians in this country are struggling with some form of duplicity in their lives. And I think, like me, what they are really wrestling with is letting go of control.

Surrender is scary, so we keep holding on. To what, I don't know ... but most of us are white knuckling it through life, holding on to the myth of control. While that box full of "adult entertainment" had ensnared me using lust, **what it actually taught me was how to justify sin in my life.** And while I would temporarily escape from the pull of the box and of pornography in general, it wouldn't be the last time I would find myself playing the justification game.

One of the reasons I escaped the pull of pornography for a season was the I got old enough to actually meet real girls ... like in person and stuff. Lots of girls. I entered each relationship with standards of purity in mind ... things I just wouldn't do ... places I just wouldn't compromise. But with each successive relationship, the line moved a little. With each relationship, I justified something new. At this point, I was a veritable expert at this point. The enemy didn't have to whisper in my ear, "Did God really say..." I was whispering those lies to myself. I can only describe this season of my life as full of tension. I was hiding things from my parents, lying to them to be able to spend time with these girls. Part of me was trying to still do the right thing. The other part of me was a teenage boy. I was constantly bouncing back and forth between the exhilaration of the taste of "forbidden fruit" and the shame of my spiritual nakedness that followed.

But I hadn't cross THAT line. I hadn't fully given myself to anyone yet. Somehow, I convinced myself that meant I was on the right side of God's line. I know now that God doesn't look at me this way. No one is on the right side of the line. Rather than holding up a measuring stick to my behavior, I think the heart of my heavenly Father was breaking as he watched me compromise what we had for something of much less value. Slowly, imperceptibly, I was losing something very important to me.

Then I met her.

I remember the night I ended up at her doorstep. I was there as a favor to a friend. His girlfriend had sent him to this address to pick something up or something. I don't actually remember the details of the situation. All I know is it wasn't my deal ... I was just riding shotgun. When the door to that house opened, there was a girl standing in front of me that took my breath away. To be fair, she wasn't the "prettiest" girl I had ever met. But to me, she was breathtaking ... literally. I could not speak. I could not move. I had never felt this way before.

Once we were safely back in my friend's car, I told him what had just happened to me. I had to know this girl. I had to get her number. I had to have her as a part of my life. After some finagling, he got me her number, and after dialing and hanging up about twenty times, I finally built up the courage to call her.

We dated for two years. I was convinced very early on this was the person I would spend my life with. Until she dumped me. My heart broken, I stumbled through a series of relationships full of regrets. I ended up at Bartlesville Wesleyan College studying for the ministry while hiding a pornography addiction that had reared its ugly head again.

Duplicity.

As a graduation gift, my parents had bought me a Sony Vaio laptop, THE laptop to have in the fall of 1997. At a time when computers were becoming a necessity at college, I had a leg up being able to have one in my room. But what I also had was a portal into my old addiction. I would spend mornings in class, afternoons writing papers for classes like Philosophy of Christian Thought and Old Testament, and evenings downloading illegal music on Napster and surfing the web for things I had no business searching for. That computer became my new box. And that box became a prison. Eventually, I would run from the shame, from my call, and from my faith.

I spent that summer diving head-first into a world I had avoided for most of my life. I had taken back control. I had given my life to God, and then I had snatched it back. That summer is a blur of bad choices. And with every bad choice came another wave of shame and regret. And with each wave, I became convinced there was nothing worth protecting. By the end of that summer, I didn't have anything left to protect. I felt like God had to be done with me. I had grabbed for control. Like Adam and Eve in the garden, my eyes had been open, and I found myself hiding.

Sin left me feeling completely and utterly exposed.

Now, I feel like I could write another entire book on my personal redemption story. That's for another day. But here I sit all these years later—happily married, three amazing kids, having served as a pastor for basically my entire adult life, and writing a book about my story (and honestly, about your story as well). I am evidence that redemption is possible and that no one is too far gone.

But instead of diving into that, I want to again use the reality of my story and my struggle as a metaphor for human spirituality. As I observe the landscape of modern Christianity ... as I look across my congregation and see so many people for whom Christianity is so much more of a struggle than it is meant to be ... I'm struck just how similar it all seems to the journey I went on. I'm living out my faith journey with a freedom I don't think most Christians ever experience. And it's not because I'm just better at this whole faith thing—so far from it. It's because I finally understand the kind of relationship I'm actually in.

When I look at Christian culture right now, I see myself. For most people, I think faith feels like my old life—a combination of technically following most of the rules, mixed with a justification of certain behaviors, topped off with a constant fear of being exposed. We live out our faith as if we are constantly afraid people are going to find out who we really are. We know the stuff that happens behind closed doors. We know who we are in the dark when no one is looking. We want what God is offering, but we struggle to count the cost of actually going all in on this relationship. It's hard to live with hidden sin in our lives ... that type of "freedom" isn't free—it comes at a massive cost. But we keep paying it. We keep wrapping up the debt of a duplicitous life because we have convinced ourselves the life God is calling us into comes as too high a cost. In the words of G.K. Chesterton:

> *"The Christian ideal has not been tried and found wanting. It has been found difficult; and left untried."*

What if the reason most people struggle with faith is not because it's too hard but because they've settled for less than the real thing? What if the weight so many people feel trying to live out their faith isn't from the weight of the cross of Christ but from the weight of our duplicitous lifestyles? What if living in Christ is (like He promised us in the gospels) "easy" and the burden truly is "light"? What if acting like a Christian is unimaginably heavy and burdensome but a life actually lived in Christ is where true freedom is found?

Let's go back to our analogy of marriage one more time. What's more difficult—waking up every day and choosing to be fully faithful to your spouse—all in, no secrets, fully surrendered ... OR ... PRETENDING to be faithful to your spouse while having a secret affair and a second life you are balancing on the side? Seems pretty obvious, doesn't it? Faithfulness is incredibly COSTLY, but it leads to a life that's so much better.

Ultimately, this is an illustration of how most people are living out their faith. I have done more weddings at this point than I can count or keep track of, which means I have filled out more marriage certificates than I can keep track of. One thing that has always struck me is a choice that every couple has to make on the certificate. Really, by hiring me, they are claiming they have made their choice ... but I'm the one who actually checks the box. It sort of reminds me of that note from elementary school with a question and two answers to choose from. Here's the question on the marriage license:

What type of ceremony is this?

- **Religious**
- **Civil**

It's strange to me this question even exists. Marriage is, at its core, a religious ceremony. The origins of marriage trace back to scripture and, again, to God's love for His bride, the church. Marriage between a man and a woman is meant to serve as a symbol of that love relationship between the almighty Bridegroom and His sometimes less than beautiful bride. By inviting and involving me in the marriage ceremony, couples are indicating they would like their wedding to be a religious ceremony. I wish more of them treated their marriage as equally divine. Sadly, most couples have a religious wedding but treat their marriage like a civil affair. While their wedding SCREAMS covenant, the marriage is lived out like a contractual obligation.

Is it any wonder, given the analogies surrounding faith and the bride of Christ, that most people who claim to be "Christians" treat faith the same way? While most people can point to a moment when they "became a Christian," they are referring to a religious ceremony:

- "I prayed a prayer to put my faith in Jesus."
- "I was baptized as a baby."

- "I went through confirmation."
- "I was raised in the church as a kid."

All of these are representative of a moment when people felt somehow "contractually obligated" to a local church, a denomination, or to the title "Christian." But faith isn't much more to most people than this—just a contractual obligation.

Faith is a covenant, but we treat it like a contractual obligation.

So what's the difference? I'm going to define our terms in just a moment, but first, one more story. I mentioned earlier in the book that I had a ring on layaway for a girl before I met Stephani. (It wasn't any of those girls I mentioned during my wandering summer OR the girl who broke my heart. I know ... I had a problem.) My friend's dad was one of the pastors at our church and was, in a lot of ways, like a second father to me. So when I met Steph and I was wrestling with all of the confusion and all my feelings, I asked him what I should do. I already had the ring for someone (a girl he knew well who also attended our church), but I couldn't deny what I was feeling for Steph. It was something more real than any other relationship I had been in. I remember sitting in Jeff's office that day. He leaned back in his chair, sighed deeply, and sat silently for what seemed to be an awkwardly long amount of time. And when he leaned forward, he changed my life.

"Phill, it's hard when you have two people you love who love you. But that's not what you have. The girl you have the ring for—she thinks she loves you. And maybe she does, but really what she has for you isn't love, it's infatuation. She's crazy about you. She would let you get away with anything in your marriage. She'd bend over backward for you. She'd give you everything, even if you didn't return the favor. But Steph—well, Steph loves you. She's equally as crazy about you, but I've seen her with you—and she won't compromise for you. She won't let you get away with things. She loves you enough that she's willing to call you on your crap. She doesn't just see who you are ... she sees who you could become, and she wants that for you. She loves you, and I think you love her, too."

He was right. Boy was he right. Now, you might be wondering what any of that has to do with defining our terms. But I think it's important before we DO define our terms that you have context for the definitions. Here's what you have to understand about the love of God:

God isn't infatuated with you. He LOVES you.

He loves you so much He sent His son, Jesus, to die for you. He loves you so much that before the foundations of the earth were laid, God had already determined you were worth it, and Jesus was already willing to go to the cross for you. God so loved the world that He sent His son, Jesus, that whoever believes in Him will not perish but will have everlasting life. But He also loves you enough to call you on your crap. He won't compromise for you. He won't let you get away with things. He can't let sin slide. He doesn't just see who you are ... He sees who you could become, and He wants that for you. He loves you. And He wants you to love Him, too. And that's why He doesn't settle for contractual obligation. That's why He invites you into a covenantal relationship. So what's the difference? I went to Merriam Webster's dictionary to define our terms:

> *Contract definition: A binding agreement between two or more persons or parties, especially one legally enforceable. A business arrangement for the supply of goods or services at a fixed price.*

The key thing to take away from this is that contracts bind two people legally, but they are missing the relational aspect of things. Contracts are, by nature, about protecting MY interests. To look at your faith as a "get out of jail free" card or "fire insurance" against hell is to treat it as a contract. To see faith as an arrangement between you and God where you accept Him as your Savior, or go to confirmation, or show up at church on Christmas and Easter, and now He is contractually obligated to let you into heaven—that somehow He OWES you—this is treating faith like a contractual obligation.

Covenants are so much more. I have to share several definitions of covenant because one can't fully capture what a covenantal relationship with God truly entails:

> **Merriam Webster:** A *usually formal, solemn, and binding agreement.*
> **Dictionary.com:** *an agreement, usually formal, between two or more persons to do or not do something specified.*

So far, this sounds a whole lot like a contract, except perhaps where Webster describes it as solemn and binding. But let's keep digging a bit. In an article written by Fuller Seminary professor, Thomas R. Schreiner, on crossway.org titled "10 Things you should know about the Biblical Covenants," we read this definition:

> **Crossway.org:** *Covenant can be defined as follows: a covenant is a chosen relationship in which two parties make binding promises to each other. (Key phrase - to each other).*

And Professor Schreiner expands on that idea in the article:

> *A covenant should be distinguished from a contract because it is a personal relationship which people voluntarily enter.*

Christopher Watkin, in his book on *Biblical Critical Theory*, expands this idea even further, noting the relational difference between covenants and contracts:

> *When we look at the nature of modern contracts and God's*

covenants with his people, we see some striking differences: God's covenants institute binding relationships, and contracts are a convenient agreement. In both relational nature and binding quality, God's covenants overflow the predetermined or calculated limits characteristic of contracts.

So we are starting to develop a picture here. While contracts are self-protecting, covenants are mutual. They contain promises made TO each other and FOR each other. They are less obligatory and more relational in nature. And they are something each party enters on their own volition—they are there because they want to be ... because they choose to be.

Catholic youth pastor Mike Landry, in his blog on mikeisthird.com, doubled down on this thinking, pushing the picture even further:

What is a covenant? Quite often, we use the word covenant interchangeably with the word contract ... the difference between the biblical understanding of "covenant" and our use of "contract" is like the difference between prostitution (as a contract) and marriage (as a covenant). Certainly, a man and a prostitute may engage in the same act as a man and his wife – but the difference in relationship is tremendous. Likewise, covenants are very different than contracts. While a contract involves a promise and an exchange of goods, a covenant involves an oath (swearing oneself) and an exchange of persons.

This tracks with the heartbeat of this entire book. We are settling for so much less than all this relationship with God is and all it has to offer because we are approaching God and a relationship with God as if it's a contractual obligation. Henri Nouwen describes this vain pursuit beautifully in his *Bread for the Journey* devotional:

When God makes a covenant with us, God says: "I will love

you with an everlasting love. I will be faithful to you, even when you run away from me, reject me, or betray me." In our society we don't speak much about covenants; we speak about contracts. When we make a contract with a person, we say: "I will fulfill my part as long as you fulfill yours. When you don't live up to your promises, I no longer have to live up to mine." Contracts are often broken because the partners are unwilling or unable to be faithful to their terms. But God didn't make a contract with us; God made a covenant with us, and God wants our relationships with one another to reflect that covenant.

So many so-called "Christians" are in it for what we can get out of it ... nothing more. We aren't Christians because we are in love with Jesus Christ or because we want to honor our heavenly Father. We are in it to protect our own interests. Faith isn't about love for us ... it's about control. We are trying to control the outcome of our lives. We are trying to navigate that fine line between getting into heaven and living the life we want to live on this earth. We are asking questions like, "What do I have to do to be saved?" and "How much faith is enough faith?" We are trying to figure out what this contract requires of us.

And that is why we miss all God has for us.
How sad.

I used to wonder what Jesus meant in Matthew 7:21-23 when He claimed that not everyone who calls Him Lord will enter the kingdom of heaven:

21 *Not everyone who calls out to me, "Lord! Lord!" will enter the Kingdom of Heaven. Only those who actually do the will of my Father in heaven will enter.* 22 *On judgment day many will say to me, "Lord! Lord! We prophesied in your name and cast out demons in your name and performed many miracles in your name."* 23 *But I will reply, "I never knew you.*

Get away from me, you who break God's laws." (Matthew 7:21-23 NLT)

This used to confuse me. It doesn't anymore. I have learned the difference between the relationship we want to have with God and the one He is inviting us into. I have learned the difference between treating my faith relationship as a contract and entering into a powerful and beautiful and holy covenant with my heavenly Father. If you look closely at these verses, you can see the problem illustrated clearly. It's not enough to call out "Lord, Lord." The differentiator is those who actually do the will of the Father. And what is God's will?

> [38] *For I have come down from heaven to do the will of God who sent me, not to do my own will.* [39] *And this is the will of God, that I should not lose even one of all those he has given me, but that I should raise them up at the last day.* [40] *For it is my Father's will that all who see his Son and believe in him should have eternal life. I will raise them up at the last day."* (John 6:38-40 NLT)

God's will for you is that through Jesus Christ, this relationship that was broken by sin would be restored to the way it was always meant to be. Over and over in scripture, God makes promises to us that are reflections of His love for us ... for you. All He is asking in return is that you chase after Him the same way He has been chasing after you. In the last chapter, we are going to look closer at that pursuit. Over and over, we see God making covenants with His people, and over and over, we see them fail to keep up their end of the bargain. But God has never given up. And it's through Jesus that the final covenant has been made. All He's waiting for is for you to join Him in that covenantal relationship through Jesus Christ. It will cost so much more than casual church attendance and Christmas and Easter appearances. It'll cost everything. And it's worth it.

CHAPTER 10

The Gift of Covenant

The costly relationship we are invited into and why it's always worth it.

Growing up in the church, I was submerged most of my life in those basic biblical stories every church teaches to their children. I grew up in the era where Sunday school was still a thing, complete with felt board Jesus and his compadres (if you know, you know). In our Sunday school classes, I got a healthy dose of what I assume were the standard stories we teach our children—stories about Adam and Eve, Noah, Moses, David and Goliath, Daniel and the Lion's Den, and even Zacchaeus, who evidently was a "wee little man" yet still had some mad tree-climbing skills. I'm thankful for the biblical foundation I got when I was a child.

But looking back, I feel like we had a tendency to whitewash the stories a little to make them a little more "age appropriate" for the kiddies. And while, as a father, I understand the logic in this thinking for sure, it did leave me with a less than complete picture of these major stories and of scripture in general. And what's worse—we never grew out of the trend ... of whitewashing the stories, that is. Yes, we spiced up our sermons with a bit more of the gory details to keep interest piqued (Adam and Eve were naked ... David cut that giant's head off ... stuff like that). But thinking back over the years, what I feel got whitewashed in all the preaching to adults was the part about what was required of me. I heard loads of sermons on God's grace and how if we confess our sins, He is faithful and just to forgive us. I heard about how no sinner is too far gone for God. I heard about how Christ laid down His life for us while we were still sinners. Powerful and profound stuff, no doubt. And every word of it absolutely true.

But what I don't remember hearing nearly as many sermons on were the passages that talked about what my faith would cost me. I don't remember hearing a whole lot of stories on surrender and self-sacrifice. On denying myself, taking up my cross daily, and following Jesus. I remember lots of sermons on Paul's missionary journeys but far too few on his shipwrecks, imprisonment, and beatings. As a result, I grew up in a generation of church attenders who were big on God's grace but whose faith fell apart the first time anything difficult happened because "The God I know would never let this happen." Um ... yes, He would. Have you read your Bible? Like ... at all?

The deeper I dove into the scriptures, particularly as I began to study for ministry, the more I realized that the church had, perhaps unintentionally but still effectively, been selling the people a spiritual bill of goods. We were great and giving half the gospel because we knew people struggled with the cost of following. What we ended up with was more attenders but less disciples and almost no disciple-makers. And when COVID-19 hit our world, we ended up with less of everything. In a vain attempt to recapture lost ground, many churches have watered the gospel down even more. But I'm finding that in the face of a global pandemic, people weren't reassured by or attracted to a faith that asked less, expected less, and inevitably MEANT less than it ever had before. The greatest gift I found we could give people was not to lower the bar. It wasn't to make it easier. It was to call them into something more real. Gone were the days when people would even make a contractual agreement with God. Many have walked away from faith completely. But many more have come looking for something real. And instead of yet again offering a cheap substitute, we have found in our local context that a far better gift is to teach our people about the reality of the relationship God really wants and the true cost of entering into this covenant.

What most people and even most Christians fail to realize is that from the creation of the world and from the first stumble of humanity into sin, God has been offering to restore this covenant relationship. The problem is that our perspective on life is too small to see the big picture. We read scripture in segments and out of context, applying its truth to our lives like it's a horoscope in the local paper or a fortune hidden inside an after-dinner cookie at the local Chinese restaurant. Our minds are trained to live life within our current reality. Even in the secular world, there has been a great devaluing of history. We live within the realm of the fifteen minutes that just happened, the present moment I am in, and the fifteen minutes that are coming. Our life is defined by sound bites. As a result, it's almost impossible for us to see the bigger picture of ... well ... anything. J.I Packer sums it up well for us:

God's covenant of grace in Scripture is one of those things that are too big to be easily seen, particularly when one's mind is programmed to look at something smaller.

And that's exactly how we have been programmed. Our world is getting smaller. Our thinking is getting smaller. Our perspective is getting smaller. The idea of a transcendent and all-powerful God doesn't compute in a mind inundated with what's right in front of me—the whole world at my fingertips. And so in so many ways in life, we continue to settle for less. And all the time, the God who made us is calling us into so much more. He's calling us into the deep. Into the fullness of all He is. And into a relationship with our creator.

To God, this has always been deeply personal.

From the very beginning, this has been about relationships. And from the very beginning, God has been extending to humanity the opportunity to join Him, not in an obligatory contractual agreement but in a meaningful and powerful covenantal relationship. Scholars continue to argue as to the exact number of covenants we see in scripture. But what they all agree on is that from the moment humanity was created and the clock started ticking, God has been offering us all of Himself and has been asking for all of us in return.

Now, you might be asking yourself—"why does this stuff even matter to us? Why are you putting so much stress on this idea of covenant?" And yet, it's precisely because we have lost sight of the value of covenantal relationship that we have continued to settle for so much less than all God is offering and all that He is asking. In an article released in January 2023 by the editorial staff of Christianity.com, they stress deeply the nature of covenants and why they should mean so much to each and every one of us.

Everything that God does is based on covenant. And when you take the bible, it's divided into two parts, the Old Tes-

tament or the Old Covenant and the New Testament or the New Covenant. So he is the God of covenants, he is the sovereign administrator of covenants.

Covenants are, in a sense, the language God uses to speak to us. The Bible is essentially a story of God making promises that He keeps and us making promises to Him that we break. And while the covenantal language in scripture can often confuse the casual reader, they deserve a closer look. And while covenants may seem archaic and out of date, it is by the grace of God that He still today offers each of us his FINAL covenant, signed and sealed by the blood of His son, Jesus, on the cross.

Covenants should matter to us because the last one listed involves everyone today. Through Jesus' sacrifice, we can become God's people. But covenants also show God's true and loyal nature. If He says he will do something, He will not break that promise. We can also see God's faithful fulfillment of the other covenants, even when humans sinned and didn't hold up their end of the oath. Praise the Lord that we have such a wonderful God who will also fulfill his covenants and promises. (christianity.com editorial staff)

And this is the story of history. As we travel together through a quick overview of the biblical covenants, you will watch history repeat itself. You will see God's faithful fulfillment of His part of the covenant. And you will see humanity fail again and again to keep up our end of the bargain. Over and over, we sin. Over and over, we break our promises. And over and over, He continues to choose us while we continue to settle for so much less than all He is offering. Obviously, where all of this is heading is to Jesus. But we've got a long way to go before we get there. So buckle up as we go on a whirlwind journey together.

As we begin our journey, I want you to have a solid overview of the components of a biblical covenant. In the book *Locat-*

ing Atonement, Author Jeremy R. Treat contributes a chapter on atonement and covenant in which he masterfully outlines four key aspects of biblical covenants. What follows will be a summary for our purposes, just to give us some context for the rest of our conversation:

First, covenants are relational.

As we have mentioned already, covenants are MORE than contracts. In Treat's description, he describes covenants as similar to a contract in their *legality* but exceeding a contract *relationally*.

In plain English, with covenants, it's all about the relationships. The promises you make in a covenant, you make because of the value you place on the relationship. Treat goes on to explain how contracts are typically focused on THINGS, but covenants are focused on PEOPLE. Contracts are about the benefits you get out of the agreement. Covenants are a measure of the depth of intimacy in the relationship between the two individuals in the covenant agreement. Again, the cultural practice of marriage is a perfect example. While most treat marriage like a contract, it truly is meant to be a covenant between two people and ultimately between those people and God. A covenant is, at its core, about relationships. Which leaves us with the question: What kind of relationship is it?

Second, covenants are familial.

Treat describes a covenant as a "*binding relationship that makes two parties as close as family*." It's the language God uses in describing marriage, where two who are previously unrelated become family by choice. (Mal. 2:14; Gen. 2:24.) Imagine that. God. Sovereign and holy God. Creator of the universe. Almighty. All-powerful. All-knowing. Ever present. Outside of time. The one who spoke the universe into existence. The God who breathed breath into Adam's lungs and brought about life as we know it. He wants a relationship with you. And not just ANY relationship—a bonding, familial, mutually beneficial relationship. Treat claims that when God chooses to enter into a covenant relationship with humanity, He is in a very real sense binding himself to them. Scripture talks often about adoption to sonship. There is an element to adoption that in a sense sets it apart from just being born into a family. In no way is it better, but it is in every way unique. As an adopted child and as a father of an adopted child, I know this firsthand. That unique element is the reality of being chosen. Biblical covenants are one way God declares to each of us—I choose you. Treat calls a covenant with God a "*kinship bond based not on natural relations but on elected relationship—on two parties choosing to be like family.*"

This covenant is not something God enters into lightly. When He makes promises to you, He means it. The invitation is to make promises in return ... and to actually mean what you say. It is an invitation to choose a familial relationship with the one who gave you life.

Third, covenants are obligational.

Covenants are promises you intend to keep. But here's the deal—I think we always intend to keep our promises. But we rarely do. Good intentions and all that. Call it a "willing spirit, weak flesh" situation. Whatever reason you want to give for it, we are pros at making promises we have every intention of keeping and then pros at making excuses why we didn't or couldn't or wouldn't keep those promises. God knew this about us. He knows our weaknesses. So to keep us honest, the invitation into covenant comes with certain obligations and with both blessings for keeping up your end of the bargain and curses for failing to do so. Every covenant carries with it language about what happens if you break the covenant. But rarely do we read the fine print. I think a lot of Christians are feeling the burden and weight of those curses even now.

Fourth, covenants are binding.

Treat uses the word "oath" to describe the nature of what we are making when we enter into a covenant relationship with God. When you get into this thing with Jesus, you are making a declarative commitment to keep the obligations of the covenant. And while that binding language can often feel daunting from our end, it is absolutely necessary. Think of this word as applied not just to you but also to God Himself. Yes, entering into a covenant relationship with God is meant to bind you to your end of the deal. But it also binds Him to you despite all the times you fall short. It binds Him to His promise to never leave you nor forsake you.

> *The greatest need of sinners is to be reconciled to God, to be brought into a covenantal relationship with their Creator.*

Not only does a covenant relationship with God bind us to Him; it is also meant to bind us to one another as members of the body of Christ. As we are about to see in our journey we are about to embark on, this covenant God is offering has both a personal element and a corporate element, binding us to the church.

> *The nature of covenants in Scripture, as both individual and corporate, can help overcome what often masquerades as a false dichotomy between the individual and the community. In Scripture, God's covenants are with a people (corporate) but make room for individual and corporate responsibility, individual and corporate guilt, and individual and corporate atonement.*

Bottom line: God is calling us into more. What these four pictures of covenant describe is a relationship with God that is so much deeper than the one most Christians are living in and settling for. The reason this book merits writing in the first place is because of just how widespread it is within Christianity to claim the name of Christ but choose less than a covenantal relationship with our Savior. We settle for so much less than all of Jesus because we think less is more. But we're not reading the fine print.

Now that we have our heads around the basic idea of a covenantal relationship, I want to trace this pattern through the entire Bible of God reaching out to humanity, offering us all of Himself in a covenant promise, only to have humans fail to hold up our end of the deal. Again, there is some argument among scholars as to just how many biblical covenants there are. This confusion only exists due to God's amazing graciousness in offering Himself to humanity again and again. Typically, most scholars agree on either six or seven covenants. We will be looking at the six that are almost universally agreed upon. O. Palmer Robinson, in his book *The Christ of the Covenants*, outlines these six covenants, giving each of them a title. I found these titles useful in helping us lock on to a picture of each covenant. They are as follows:

- **Adam:** the covenant of commencement
- **Noah:** the covenant of preservation
- **Abraham:** the covenant of promise
- **Moses:** the covenant of law
- **David:** the covenant of the kingdom
- **Christ:** the covenant of consummation

Adam: The Covenant of Commencement

There is a lot of argument about whether this one counts, as Adam didn't really have a lot of say in being created in God's image and having the breath of life breathed into Him. And yet there is a lot of value in viewing this as a covenant God was making at creation. As you watch Adam and Eve be given instruction in the garden, given dominion over the animals, given a job to tend to the earth ... and eventually given a choice between following God and choosing their own path ... all the elements of covenant seem to be present, particularly the element of relationship. God has Adam name all the animals, but none of them are found to be a suitable helper for him. None are a good fit. So God creates Eve and by doing so creates a covenantal bond between these two humans that for eternity is meant to serve as a reflection of the bond He wants with us. And God's covenant promises to us are caught up in Adam's relationship with Eve.

> *God makes a covenant with Adam (mediator), promising a fruitful union and the blessing of offspring; the condition is that they not eat from the tree of the knowledge of good and evil. The sign of this covenant is the Sabbath day, celebrated by one holy couple.* (Pastor Mike Landry)

This was God's plan. This was God's promise. And Adam and Eve made their promise to God as well. And for a while, everything was great. They walked with God in the garden in perfect union. And as we talked about at the beginning of the book, they were naked and knew no shame. But Adam and Eve were the first to do what humanity has a track record of doing. They settle for less than all of God.

> *The serpent was the shrewdest of all the wild animals the Lord God had made. One day he asked the woman, "Did God really say you must not eat the fruit from any of the trees in the garden?"* [2] *"Of course we may eat fruit from the trees in the garden," the woman replied.* [3] *"It's only the fruit from the tree in the middle of the garden that we are not allowed to eat. God said, 'You must not eat it or even touch it; if you do, you will die.'"* [4] *"You won't die!" the serpent replied to the woman.* [5] *"God knows that your eyes will be opened as soon as you eat it, and you will be like God, knowing both*

good and evil." [6] *The woman was convinced. She saw that the tree was beautiful and its fruit looked delicious, and she wanted the wisdom it would give her. So she took some of the fruit and ate it. Then she gave some to her husband, who was with her, and he ate it, too.* [7] *At that moment their eyes were opened, and they suddenly felt shame at their nakedness. So they sewed fig leaves together to cover themselves.* (Genesis 3:1-7 NLT)

God gave Adam and Eve a choice. They chose poorly. They turned away. They broke the covenant. And in doing so, they fractured relationships as we know them. Sandra Richter describes this fracture so well in her book:

Adam's breach with the Father has also fractured humanity's relational world. Self-centeredness and competition are now the relational norms. A healthy relationship, at any level, is hard to find.

Whitney Woollard from the Bible Project doubles down on this notion:

And in their first test of covenant faithfulness, humans failed. They ate from the tree, fracturing the human-divine relationship and plunging humanity into corruption and death. We'd still be stuck in the wreckage if God never intervened. But the rest of the Bible is all about how God is repairing this broken partnership with humans.

The first attempt at covenant was short-lived. We don't know exactly how long—could have been days, weeks, months, or even years. What we do know is that this would be the first domino in an ongoing story of God reaching out to humanity and humanity making promises we never keep.

Noah: The Covenant of Preservation

This idea of preservation carries with it the notion that there is something worth preserving. If you were to follow humanity from the fall of Adam and Eve into sin, forward to the time of Noah, what you would find is a world with hardly anything worth preserving:

> *After Adam and Eve's exile from Eden, the biblical narrative feels grim...Cain sides with the serpent, killing his brother in cold blood, and a man named Lamech brags about his murderous, chauvinistic ways. Genesis 5 repeats the refrain "and he died" eight times, revealing how death reigned over humanity. Then there's this weird story in Genesis 6 that's meant to show the rapid advancement of evil. So that by the time we come to the story of Noah, sin has enveloped the whole world, sending it back into pre-creation chaos. (The Five Key Covenants God Makes With Humans in the Bible: Partnerships Between God and People - Whitney Woollard)*

While Adam and Eve initially made the choice to settle for less than all of God, humanity would actually perfect it in the coming generations. And yet in the middle of all of it, God found Noah:

> [5] *The Lord observed the extent of human wickedness on the earth, and he saw that everything they thought or imagined was consistently and totally evil.* [6] *So the Lord was sorry he had ever made them and put them on the earth. It broke his heart.* [7] *And the Lord said, "I will wipe this human race I have created from the face of the earth. Yes, and I will destroy every living thing—all the people, the large animals, the small animals that scurry along the ground, and even the birds of the sky. I am sorry I ever made them."* [8] *But Noah found favor with the Lord. (Genesis 6:5-8 NLT)*

God tests Noah before making any promises. In the face of immense persecution and mockery, Noah builds a giant boat in the middle of the desert. He spends his life working on what feels like a fruitless task and begging people to turn to God. In the end, no one joins him on the boat but his family and two of each animal. Ironically, the animals listened to God, but the people did not. The storm comes, humanity is given a hard reboot, and only after all of this does God make a covenant with Noah.

> *Then God blessed Noah and his sons and told them, "Be fruitful and multiply. Fill the earth. [2] All the animals of the earth, all the birds of the sky, all the small animals that scurry along the ground, and all the fish in the sea will look on you with fear and terror. I have placed them in your power. [3] I have given them to you for food, just as I have given you grain and vegetables. [4] But you must never eat any meat that still has the lifeblood in it.* (Genesis 9:1-4 NLT)

This sounds eerily similar to his original covenant with Adam and Eve. In a sense, God is re-establishing His original covenant promise. But there is a change to it. Blood has been shed. Sin has entered the world. The first covenant was made with sinless people. When Adam and Eve sinned, now sin has to be part of the equation moving forward. God killed animals and made clothing for Adam and Eve out of the skin of the animals. He gave them clothing to cover their shame, but the picture was clear. There is a price for covering shame. There is a cost for restoration of what has been lost.

Now in this covenant agreement, God is restoring a relationship with Him, but that relationship will forever have changed with the animals. Because of the shedding of blood, man is now something to fear. God has given them their part of the covenant. He then goes out to outline his own promise:

> [12] *Then God said, "I am giving you a sign of my covenant with you and with all living creatures, for all generations to come. [13] I have placed my rainbow in the clouds. It is the sign of my covenant with you and with all the earth. [14] When I send clouds over the earth, the rainbow will appear in the clouds, [15] and I will remember my covenant with you and with all living creatures. Never again will the floodwaters*

destroy all life. [16] *When I see the rainbow in the clouds, I will remember the eternal covenant between God and every living creature on earth."* [17] *Then God said to Noah, "Yes, this rainbow is the sign of the covenant I am confirming with all the creatures on earth."* (Genesis 9:12-17 NLT)

Abraham: The Covenant of Promise

Fast forward multiple generations. After God's covenant with Noah, humanity is given a second chance of sorts. And yet they continue to fail at holding up their end of the bargain. God is choosing them. They are not choosing Him back. Instead, they are choosing to chase the pleasures of this world. Genesis 9-11 records the downward spiral of humanity until, as readers, we're left wondering how this thing is ever going to turn around. Enter: Abraham.

God reached out to Abraham, yet again placing his hope in a human to try to turn this thing around. In Genesis 15-22, we read this story, and we are made aware of the terms of this covenant. God is offering nationhood; descendants so numerous they are "like the stars in the sky." He offers them a piece of "promised land" and claims that Abraham will bring a universal blessing upon humanity (Genesis 17:1-8). But this time, we see a shift in the dynamics of the covenant. Up to this point, God has promised the world, and all that has been asked in return is that we would choose Him ... that we would choose obedience. This time, God (quite literally) wants to make sure we've got some skin in the game. And, true to his nature and character, He offers us the same. First, God shows us just how serious He is about His promise:

[9] *The Lord told him, "Bring me a three-year-old heifer, a three-year-old female goat, a three-year-old ram, a turtledove, and a young pigeon."* [10] *So Abram presented all these*

to him and killed them. Then he cut each animal down the middle and laid the halves side by side; he did not, however, cut the birds in half. [11] *Some vultures swooped down to eat the carcasses, but Abram chased them away.*
[17] *After the sun went down and darkness fell, Abram saw a smoking firepot and a flaming torch pass between the halves of the carcasses.* [18] *So the Lord made a covenant with Abram that day and said, "I have given this land to your descendants, all the way from the border of Egypt to the great Euphrates River—* [19] *the land now occupied by the Kenites, Kenizzites, Kadmonites,* [20] *Hittites, Perizzites, Rephaites,* [21] *Amorites, Canaanites, Girgashites, and Jebusites." (Genesis 15:9-11, 19-21 NLT)*

Now, context in scripture is everything. So often, the things we don't understand or the things we miss in scripture come down to a lack of understanding of the context. This moment is a powerful example of just what I'm talking about. While we have no context for the cutting in half of these animals or the passing of the fireboat and torch between the animal halves, it would have spoken volumes to Abraham. To cut these animal pieces in half and walk between them was to make an oath with your life. Essentially, it was like saying, "If I don't keep up my end of the bargain, may the same thing happen to me that happened to these animals." God was sending a very clear message again—I'm all in on you.

The purpose of the cut animals, then, is to remind Abram of the seriousness with which the Lord takes the promise and the covenant commitment into which he has entered to keep his promise. (Christopher Watkin - Biblical Critical Theory: How the Bible's Unfolding Story Makes Sense of Modern Life and Culture.)

And not only that—the smoking firepot and the torch in the

darkness also paint a powerful picture we can't afford to miss and a question we all need to be willing to ask of ourselves:

> *Three physical signs of God's presence—a smoking firepot, a flaming torch and enveloping darkness—tell us everlasting truths about God. The Lord was both hidden (the darkness) and revealed (in the light). The Lord's presence, like fire, both attracts and repels. We draw near for warmth but must keep our distance, lest we be burned. God's love draws us toward him, but his holiness threatens to consume us as we come closer. In the end, it is our decision how close we come and how willing we are to risk being consumed.* (Mike Breen, *Covenant and Kingdom: The DNA of the Bible*)

But then God turns the whole deal back on Abraham in Genesis 17. In essence, He is about to ask Abraham, "Are you all in on me?" And God doesn't just want Abraham to say it. He wants Abraham to show it. But what could Abraham ever do that would even hold a candle to the promise He saw God make to Him?

> [9] *Then God said to Abraham, "Your responsibility is to obey the terms of the covenant. You and all your descendants have this continual responsibility.* [10] *This is the covenant that you and your descendants must keep: Each male among you must be circumcised.* [11] *You must cut off the flesh of your foreskin as a sign of the covenant between me and you.* [12] *From generation to generation, every male child must be circumcised on the eighth day after his birth. This applies not only to members of your family but also to the servants born in your household and the foreign-born servants whom you have purchased.* [13] *All must be circumcised. Your bodies will bear the mark of my everlasting covenant.* [14] *Any male who fails to be circumcised will be cut off from the covenant family for breaking the covenant."* (Genesis 17:9-14 NLT)

Yup. That'll do it.

Again, context is everything here. Without question, there is the obvious commitment it would take. Are you into God? PROVE IT.

But there is more to the story, and this is much more than just a bizarre request from God. Many will point to the medical benefits of circumcision, as removing the foreskin on the eighth day actually reduces all sorts of opportunity for impurity and infection. Certainly God knew this, and while this was not the point of God choosing circumcision, it actually backs and validates the point. The science behind circumcision sort of puts the exclamation point on the promise God is calling them into.

What God was speaking to in this picture is a call for His people to be faithful—not just in this present generation but for generations to come. Removing the foreskin was symbolic of cutting away the curse of the fallen sinful nature. God had promised to make Abraham a great nation. That has to start with Abraham and Sarah having a child. A child of the promise. Before that happened, God required this picture of circumcision. It was a visual way of saying to God, "I'm all in now, and I promise to pass this truth on to the next generation." Circumcision was a picture of generational faithfulness. Later, the Apostle Paul would apply this metaphor on a spiritual level.

> [28] *For you are not a true Jew just because you were born of Jewish parents or because you have gone through the ceremony of circumcision.* [29] *No, a true Jew is one whose heart is right with God. And true circumcision is not merely obeying the letter of the law; rather, it is a change of heart produced by the Spirit. And a person with a changed heart seeks praise from God, not from people.* (Romans 2:28-29 NLT)

God tells Abraham to leave his land and follow wherever he leads, train his family to do what is right and just, and practice circumcision in every generation. This covenant is both conditional and unconditional. God and Abraham each have a part to play, but ultimately, God will keep his promise to give Abraham a family who will inherit the land and bless the world.

This is the true call of circumcision and the true call of the covenant. It's God's way of asking whether or not we're all in. It requires more than words. There is a cutting away that is needed of all things impure so our heart can be only for Him. And there is a decision we each need to make about how close we will get to God and whether or not we are willing, as Mike Breen so eloquently put it, to "risk being consumed" by all of who God is.

Moses: The Covenant of Law

Exodus opens with a glimpse into God's fulfillment of His promise, as Abraham's offspring are multiplying rapidly in Egypt. This threatens the current Pharaoh, and the Egyptians end up enslaving Israel—the people of God. Perhaps for the first time, we see some very vocal questioning of God—particularly about whether or not He was keeping up His end of this covenant. Israel cries out to God for help, and scripture says He hears them. God uses Moses (an unlikely hero) to deliver the Israelites through ten plagues against the Egyptians (an unlikely plan) and then parts the Red Sea so they can cross through the sea on dry land (an unlikely escape plan). All of this leads them to the foot of Mt. Sinai, where, rather than making a completely new covenant, God sort of doubles down on the one He has already made, adding a few addendums to the agreement. The sign of the New Covenant is the Ten Commandments (see Exodus 20).

> *After a harrowing escape, the people reach the foot of Mount Sinai, where God shows up to revisit the promises he made to Abraham. Acting as the representative for Israel, Moses ascends the mountain to hear the terms of God's covenant with the people. God promises to make Israel into a holy*

kingdom of priests that will spread his blessing and glory to all the nations. God instructed Israel to obey all the laws given at Mount Sinai, promising to bring blessings if they followed his commands and curses if they ignored them (The Five Key Covenants God Makes With Humans in the Bible - Whitney Woollard)

Moses goes up the mountain and meets with God for forty days. When he returns, he has God's commands, on stone tablets, to share with the people. God had literally written His promises in stone. Sadly, Moses doesn't make it down the mountain with the Ten Commandments before Israel is already breaking the covenant. In what can only be described as a divine mulligan (if you don't know, as a golfer), God has Moses come back UP the mountain and make replacement tablets (as Moses had sort of smashed the first set in his anger). I wish I could say this set Israel on a new trajectory. Sadly, it does not. We will continue to see Israel do what humanity does—make promises they can't seem to keep.

But what I want to draw our attention to here is Moses. A little backstory on Moses. He was Israelite. He was the adopted son of the previous Pharaoh's daughter. He was raised in the palace. He grew up watching his people enslaved by the Egyptians. And his heart always broke for his people. At one point, he took matters into his own hands and ended up killing someone and having to run for his life. He lived the next forty years hiding in the desert as a lowly shepherd. And yet God used the brokenness of this season to shape Moses into someone He could use. One of my favorite D.L. Moody quotes of all time describes the life of Moses this way:

Moses spent the first 40 years thinking he was somebody. He spent the second forty years learning he was a nobody.

> *He spent his third 40 years discovering what God can do with a nobody.*

In this covenant promise, which God definitely makes with Israel, they fail miserably to hold up their end of the deal. But there is a profound lesson to be learned through Moses. Often, when we turn our back on God's covenant, it's simply because of our own flawed natures. Simply put, we want sin more than we want Him. But sometimes, perhaps more times than people care to admit, we actually struggle because we think God has failed us. If you remember back to our chapter on expectations, we have already established that we often bring unrealistic expectations to our relationship with God. When things don't go the way we want or when life is harder than we want it to be, we start to question whether God is holding up His end of the deal at all. Moses gives us a glimpse into the reality of brokenness. He shows us that even in the darkest of seasons, God is still faithful, He is still pursuing us, and He is still true to His word.

> *We may wonder if there is any purpose in the "broken" times of our life, times when we have suffered failure, loss or disappointment. The life of Moses tells us that these hurts are like instruments that God can use to shape our lives. Difficulty rather than ease fashions our character and gives us "depth." Moses embraced the conditions of his life and "went to the far side of the desert." He may have thought he was escaping only his difficult circumstances, but in fact, Moses gave God the opportunity to shape him into the man that he would become. We must do the same if we are to achieve all that God has for us. (Mike Breen, Covenant and Kingdom: The DNA of the Bible)*

David: The Covenant of the Kingdom

Eventually, God's people actually make it to the Promised Land.

It takes them a rebellion, forty years of wandering in the wilderness, and a second try under the leadership of Moses' protege, a man named Joshua. Through a series of miracles, the so-called "people of God" stumble over the finish line and into the Promised Land. But lest you are ready to celebrate their obedience, I'd hold your applause just yet.

This is the land God promised. God is, yet again, keeping up His end of the bargain. Our end of the bargain was, again, simply faithfulness. Follow the Ten Commandments. Live in the land. Purify the land from evil. Be my people, and I will be your King. Your only King. I have chosen you. Now, just choose me back.

Yet somehow, they couldn't even manage that. God was their king, so Israel was not in need of a king. So God had them appoint judges to rule over the people. This started a pattern with the Israelite people. They would promise God their faithfulness. Then they would drift. Eventually, they would find themselves off course and in over their heads. They would cry out to God. God would send a new judge, and Israel would promise God their faithfulness again. And then they would drift. And the merry-go-round would start all over again.

By the way, one of the reasons I've invested my time and my heart into writing this book is because as I survey the landscape of Christianity, this is how I see most Christians living their lives. It's almost like we don't know any different. It's almost like we are unaware this isn't how Christianity is supposed to be. It's just a merry-go-round of going my own way, asking God to bail me out, and starting all over. Just like Israel, God is supposed to be our King. As in, sovereign ruler of our lives. And yet, I think the current state of Christianity in the United States places us on similar soil as the Israelites at the end of the book of Judges. They were in the Promised Land but not living free. They had been delivered by God but were still stuck on the merry-go-round of sin and repentance. And worst of all:

> [25] *In those days Israel had no king; all the people did whatever seemed right in their own eyes.* (Judges 21:25 NLT)

This is not a reference to God's desire for them to appoint a king. It's a reference to God's desire to BE their King. And yet, like always, Israel wanted what they wanted. In 1 Samuel 8, Israel begins to look around at the world around them. They don't want to be a nation set apart for God. They want to be like everyone else. Isn't that what Christians today still struggle with? We want to be God's people, but we don't want to follow God's commands. We want to be saved, but we don't want a Savior. We want to go to heaven, but we don't want to surrender our lifestyles and freedoms here on earth. And so we try to fit God and faith into a mold that works for us in the world we are living in.

We try to fit God into a box.

That's exactly what Israel does. They begin to demand a king. And despite God's warnings through Samuel the prophet, they continue to demand their way and their version of following God. God made the covenant, but they started to try to change the rules.

> [19] *But the people refused to listen to Samuel's warning. "Even so, we still want a king," they said.* [20] *"We want to be like the nations around us. Our king will judge us and lead us into battle."* [21] *So Samuel repeated to the Lord what the people had said,* [22] *and the Lord replied, "Do as they say, and give them a king." Then Samuel agreed and sent the people home.* (1 Samuel 8:19-22 NLT)

Do you hear the language? It should ring eerily familiar in the ears of today's church. "But the people refused to listen." "We want to be like the nations around us." They were asking the question I think Christians have been asking since the fall of Adam and Eve: How can I live in God's covenant, but on my terms? And here's the honest answer ...

You can't. You can't follow God on your terms.

Saul is appointed King of Israel. He is everything THEY were looking for in a king, but eventually, his true colors would be revealed, and Israel would again be in desperate need of God's intervention. But what God does next is profound. Yet again, he makes a covenant with His people. But this time, He does it through the appointing of a new king. God moves even further toward us. He is still committed to His side of the deal, but now, He is even willing to keep His promises through the lineage of an earthly king.

But this time, it would be God and not the people who would choose the king. When Israel chose their king, they picked a guy who, from all outward appearances, was everything you would want in a king. Handsome. A head taller than anyone else. He probably even had perfect white teeth. But the part that mattered—the part you can't see—was missing. Saul didn't have a heart surrendered to God. And as time went on, his true character is exposed.

And yet as Samuel went about the process of appointing a new king, we find him looking for the exact same attributes and the exact same kind of outward appearance.

> *Now the Lord said to Samuel, "You have mourned long enough for Saul. I have rejected him as king of Israel, so fill your flask with olive oil and go to Bethlehem. Find a man named Jesse who lives there, for I have selected one of his sons to be my king." (1 Samuel 16:1 NLT)*

Samuel obeys the Lord and heads out to find Jesse's family. When he finds them, he invites them to the sacrifice ... but his real reason for inviting them is to get a closer look at these sons of Jesse to see if one of them looked like a king.

> [6] *When they arrived, Samuel took one look at Eliab and thought, "Surely this is the Lord's anointed!"* (1 Samuel 16:6 NLT)

One look. He took one look.

Samuel didn't dig deeper. Samuel didn't ask any questions. He just took one look. He saw what was on the surface, and he liked it. He knew the people would like it, too. The people were mourning the loss of Saul, and he knew Eliab would fit the bill perfectly. He would scratch the itch for the Israelites. But God calls Him out, making it clear that this time, He would be choosing the king.

> [7] *But the Lord said to Samuel, "Don't judge by his appearance or height, for I have rejected him. The Lord doesn't see things the way you see them. People judge by outward appearance, but the Lord looks at the heart."* (1 Samuel 16:7 NLT)

Eventually, God will point out David as his anointed. While he is described as "dark and handsome with beautiful eyes," it's not the outward appearance God is looking for at all. He sees into the heart of this man and finds a man who will be faithful in leading the people and who will repent when he stumbles. God doesn't find a perfect man in David. But He does find a man who will love Him back and who will lead the people to love Him back, too. Not only does David become Israel's most successful leader to date, uniting the kingdom and restoring order—he also prioritizes God in his kingship. He longs to build a temple for God so that once again, God and Israel can be in covenant relationship. God won't let him build the temple and leaves that job to David's son, Solomon. But God DOES do something pretty powerful. He makes yet another promise.

> [8] *Now go and say to my servant David, 'This is what*

the Lord of Heaven's Armies has declared: I took you from tending sheep in the pasture and selected you to be the leader of my people Israel. [9] *I have been with you wherever you have gone, and I have destroyed all your enemies before your eyes. Now I will make your name as famous as anyone who has ever lived on the earth!* (2 Samuel 7:8-9 NLT)

'Furthermore, the Lord declares that he will make a house for you—a dynasty of kings! [12] *For when you die and are buried with your ancestors, I will raise up one of your descendants, your own offspring, and I will make his kingdom strong.* [13] *He is the one who will build a house—a temple—for my name. And I will secure his royal throne forever.* 14 *I will be his father, and he will be my son. If he sins, I will correct and discipline him with the rod, like any father would do.* [15] *But my favor will not be taken from him as I took it from Saul, whom I removed from your sight.* [16] *Your house and your kingdom will continue before me for all time, and your throne will be secure forever.'* (2 Samuel 7:11b-16 NLT)

God says to David—I'm going to keep my promise through you. Salvation is going to come through your kingdom. And even though at times David and his descendants would fail to keep their part of the deal ... God never relented. He never went back on his word.

David is chosen by God to lead Israel as her King – and God swears to David that one of his descendants will forever remain on the throne of Israel. The sign of this covenant is the throne and Temple which Solomon, David's son, will build – and the nation has now become a Holy Kingdom. (Mike Breen, *Covenant and Kingdom: The DNA of the Bible*)

Hundreds of years go by ... but God never forgets His promise. And then one night in Bethlehem, the cries of a baby break through the night as, at that moment, heaven breaks through to earth, and the son of God takes on flesh. Our flesh. Joseph, the husband of Mary, was in Bethlehem that night because of a census that the Roman government had required. He had to return to Bethlehem because of his lineage—Joseph was from the line of David.

> *Now the Lord said to Samuel, "You have mourned long enough for Saul. I have rejected him as king of Israel, so fill your flask with olive oil and go to Bethlehem. Find a man named Jesse who lives there, for I have selected one of his sons to be my king."* (1 Samuel 16:1 NLT)

Jesus was born in the same small town from the same family line as King David. This shepherd turned king from the Old Testament was in every way of foreshadowing of the Messiah to come—the fulfillment of God's promise. Scholars have pointed out for centuries the similarities between David and Jesus. It's almost as if God knew what He was doing when HE chose the king! Look at just a few of these comparisons:

- Both were descended from Abraham and were from the tribe of Judah.
- David was a shepherd; Jesus describes himself as the good shepherd.
- Both were crowned king in Jerusalem.
- Both died in Jerusalem.
- Both loved God and loved the people.
- Both suffered rejection from the people they loved.
- Both were betrayed by someone close to them.
- Both wept on the Mount of Olives over the tragedies taking place in Jerusalem.
- David was a man after God's own heart; Jesus Christ WAS God's heart.

In choosing David as king, God was foreshadowing the king that would come and the kind of king who would ultimately usher in the final covenant. This entire journey and all of these covenants were ultimately pointing to and leading to one man, one moment, and one ultimate promise.

> *All of these covenants thematically build on one another. After God's covenant with David, as readers, we are left waiting for the great deliverer, the Messiah from David's line, who will make right the fractured relationship that began in the garden. (The Five Key Covenants God Makes With Humans in the Bible - Whitney Woollard)*

That's really what this has all been about. Making right that fractured relationship. Fixing what was broken. Restoring what has been lost. All through His son, Jesus. It really all comes down to Jesus. The biblical word for this is **atonement**. A simple definition of atonement is the reconciling of God and humanity through the sacrifice of Jesus Christ.

> *The doctrine of the atonement is the church's understanding of the way in which Christ, through all of his work but primarily his death, has dealt with sin and its effects in order to restore the broken covenant relationship between God and sinners and thereby establish God's redemptive rule over his creation. (Jeremy Treat - Locating Atonement)*

What does atonement have to do with God's covenant? Everything.

> *Covenant is not only indispensable context for atonement, but it is also intrinsic to the very definition of atonement. In other words, one cannot rightly understand atonement itself apart from covenant. (Jeremy Treat - Locating Atonement)*

The covenant relationship God is inviting us into is one He has been building to from the beginning of time. Atonement is what God is bringing to the table in this promise. In order to truly restore this relationship with our creator, our sin had to be atoned for—someone had to pay the price for all of our failures. Throughout the scriptures, God gave humanity a chance to prove to themselves that we can't do this on our own. Time and again, He would give us a chance. Time and again, we would fail. And this is what we all still do. We will try and fail, and try and fail ... until we ultimately reach the moment where we can admit to ourselves—I don't think I can do this on my own.

> *Do you notice how the covenants progressively build upon one another, forming a complete redemptive storyline? God preserved the world through Noah, initiated redemption through Abraham, established the nation of Israel through Moses, promised an eternal shepherd-king through David, and then fulfilled all of his covenants through Jesus. With each covenant, God's promises and plans to save the world through the seed of the woman become clearer and clearer until we finally see that redemption can only come through King Jesus. (The Five Key Covenants God Makes With Humans in the Bible - Whitney Woollard)*

That's where this is all leading. To that moment where you finally see in your life—redemption can only come through Jesus. Some people never reach that moment. Many people, actually. This is where the rubber truly meets the road in Christianity. God is about to go all in on His promise. Jesus is about to shed His blood. He will lay down His life for this covenant. And as we will see as we dive into this final covenant, signed by the blood of Jesus Christ, what God is asking for in return is for all of us. Any version of Christianity that settles for less isn't real. It's an image. A fake. It's a pin-up version of Christianity. It's lust v. love. It's contract v. covenant. You're either all in or all out. Anything less than this isn't real. **It's spiritual pornography.**

CHAPTER 11

Just Say Yes

Why you will never regret chasing all of Jesus.

> [6] *As for me, my life has already been poured out as an offering to God. The time of my death is near.* [7] *I have fought the good fight, I have finished the race, and I have remained faithful.* [8] *And now the prize awaits me—the crown of righteousness, which the Lord, the righteous Judge, will give me on the day of his return. And the prize is not just for me but for all who eagerly look forward to his appearing.* (2 Timothy 4:6–8 NLT)

Next to Jesus, there is no one in the scriptures more inspiring than the Apostle Paul. It's easy to forget that Paul used to be known as Saul—a religious leader and persecutor of Christians. He used to see Christianity as dangerous. Dangerous to his beliefs. Dangerous to his understanding of faith. Dangerous to his way of life. And he was right on all three accounts. Paul was so set on his understanding of a life of faith ... and now this group of Christians, these followers of a man named Jesus, were challenging all of it. They weren't dismissing the faith of the Jewish people per se—in actuality, they were redefining it. They were claiming this Jesus was the Messiah they had been waiting for. But He couldn't be, could He? After all, He was turning everything they believed about God ... upside down.

Saul had based his entire life on learning and following God's law. And now, these Christians were claiming Jesus came not to abolish the law but to fulfill it. They claimed true freedom was a result not of our good works but of accepting forgiveness of our sins and being "saved" by grace ... through faith in this man Jesus. God's covenant, they claimed, never had been about being good enough. It never was something you could earn. All that was needed, so they claimed, was faith. And nothing you did to try to earn your way to heaven would ever be enough. Filthy rags. They compared our good works to filthy rags. This just couldn't be. This just wouldn't work.

It took a lot to finally get ahold of Saul. It took a visit from God Himself, a flash of brilliant light, a divinely powered case of blindness on the road to Damascus (see Acts 9 in the Bible), and a voice from heaven asking Saul directly—"why are you persecuting me?"

"*Who are you ... Lord?*" was Saul's reply.

He knew whoever was speaking was divine... but realized in this moment that He had no idea who God really was. The answer from the voice changed his life forever.

"*I am Jesus ... the one you have been persecuting.*"

I am ... Jesus. This was the moment Saul realized Jesus is the son of God. It's all true. It's all real. This moment changed everything. Saul (whom we now know as the Apostle Paul) had his entire life turned upside down by one simple yet profound realization—Jesus is who he says he is.

This entire book has been about trying to get you to see that truth and to have that moment for yourself. I grew up, as I've previously mentioned, in a Christian and yet somewhat legalistic home. I prayed the prayer to accept Jesus when I was young. That day, when I stood over "the box," feeling the magnetic pull of the temptation and the choice it represented in my life, I knew what I was choosing was wrong. I knew what Jesus had done for me on the cross. I knew what sin was and how it separates us from God. And like Adam and Eve, I believed the lies of the enemy—you won't surely die! Why would a good God keep this from you? Lust of the eyes. Lust of the flesh. The pride of life. Like Eve, I reached for the forbidden fruit, desperate to taste its sweetness. And though there was shame and hiding that followed, over time, the shame decreased, the justifying increased, and before I knew it, I was at Bartlesville Wesleyan College, studying for ministry and yet hiding from God, covering my nakedness with the fig leaves formed from all the things I knew I was supposed to be publicly. Maybe you've got your own version of this story.

Sadly, it took me far too long to figure it out. And sadly, it took a Damascus road moment in my life, too. I left college after my freshman year with no plans of returning. I turned my back on my calling. I turned my back on the church. I turned my back on God. I fully embraced everything I had been hiding in the dark. My secret sins became my lifestyle. I lost my way. I reaped what I had been secretly sowing. I lost my virginity. I lost my hope and purpose in life. I tried to find my way through drugs and alcohol. I tried to find purpose in relationship after relationship. I hurt people, particularly girls, that I treated not as image bearers of God but the same way I had treated those images that came out of the box—as if they were there for my pleasure. By the end of the summer, I didn't know who I was anymore. All I knew is that I was miserable. I had thrown away my faith and walked away from my relationship with my heavenly Father. I was lost.

The day of my Damascus road experience, I remember waking up in my bed at my parents' house. I mention I remember waking up there because I don't remember getting there. In fact, I don't remember much of anything from the night before, and what I do remember would make you blush. I believe the Holy Spirit woke me up that morning at 6:15 a.m. Sun was pouring through my window, warming my face, reminding me what hope felt like and also how little of it I actually had. I surveyed my room and found it was littered with passed-out people. Some I knew. Some I didn't. I didn't remember coming home. I didn't remember being with these people. Not friends. People. I knew clearly in my heart—these were not friends. Not real ones anyway. As I lay there feeling about as lost as I have ever remembered feeling, I heard the voice of God's Holy Spirit. Only a few times in my life can I say I actually "heard" the voice of God. I would often read something in His word and it would speak to me, or I would get a sense of conviction in my spirit about something. But rarely was it an audible voice. THAT morning, the Holy Spirit spoke to me.

So the answer to hypocrisy is hypocrisy.
Interesting.

That's all He said. That's all He needed to say. I knew exactly what He meant. I had spent the entire year previous collecting evidence of all the ways the Christians around me were hypocritical in their faith—claiming one thing but falling short. I was looking for evidence. I was looking for excuses. I was looking for a reason to run. But in that moment that morning in my bed in my parents' home, I didn't have to ask, "Who are you, Lord?" I knew. I knew how much I had let Him down. I knew how lost I was. I knew I had made a huge mistake. But more importantly, I knew something I think deep down I had always known, although in that moment of clarity, I was owning for the first time.

I've never loved Jesus back.

I mean ... not really anyway. I'd had moments where I felt the emotions and the feels. I'd spent a lot of my life trying to live by the rules and knowing right from wrong and how God wanted me to live. I was a Bible quiz master—so I knew the answers. But I don't think I ever truly knew Jesus. I found myself wondering what this Christianity thing would be like if I actually just committed my life to Jesus completely. I had accepted Him as Savior. What would happen if I actually surrendered to Him as Lord? I didn't know for sure ... but I wanted to find out. In that moment ... like Saul, I felt the scales fall off my eyes ... and for the first time, I got a glimpse of the goodness of Jesus. And like Saul (whom we now know as the Apostle Paul), I quit looking at this faith thing as a contractual obligation, and I entered fully into a covenant relationship with Jesus Christ, my Savior. And life has never been the same.

This covenant I'm talking about is different than the covenants we covered in Chapter 10. It's more. Now, in no way am I suggesting that in any of the biblical covenants that God did less than all of what He promised. He was never the problem. We were. But in this final covenant, signed with the blood of His son, Jesus, on the cross, God not only did our part ... He let Jesus do our part. And while this relationship with God still costs us ... well ... everything, what Jesus did for us on the cross paid a price we were simply incapable of paying. Through His sacrifice, Jesus made it possible for my life to be ... enough. So let's take a closer look at this New Covenant, made possible through Jesus Christ.

In my research, I found several references to Jesus as the "**Covenantal Climax**." I think that hits it right on its head. As you look back across the landscape of the first covenants, you realize just how profound Jesus was. Nowhere did I find a better snapshot of this than from Whitney Woollard of The Bible Project:

> *The New Testament authors present Jesus as the offspring of Abraham who trusted Yahweh, even to the point of death, and became a blessing to all nations. He is the greater* Moses, *leading us out of bondage, and he is the obedient Israelite who perfectly follows the laws of God. He is the royal son of David who inaugurated God's Kingdom in his life, death, and resurrection, and who now sits at God's right hand forever reigning as the one true King. Jesus perfectly succeeded at every point where humanity failed. He is the guarantor and mediator of the new and better covenant* (Heb. 7:22, 9:15). *Now people from every nation, tribe, and tongue who trust Jesus can become a part of God's covenant family. In the new covenant, we receive the forgiveness of sins and God's empowering Spirit to help us live lives full of self-giving love. Because of Jesus, we can live righteously and partner with him as he renews the world.*

And where did this all start? At the beginning. Interestingly enough, Jesus is also often referred to as the **second Adam**. The reality is, before the first Adam was ever created and before God breathed breath into the lungs of humanity, He knew the second Adam would be needed. In John's gospel, as he recounts the story of Jesus, he doesn't start at the birth of Jesus as a human. He goes back before the creation of the world and reminds us of a powerful truth:

> *In the beginning the Word* [that's Jesus] *already existed. The Word was with God, and the Word was God.* [2] *He existed in the beginning with God.* [3] *God created everything through him, and nothing was created except through him.* [4] *The Word gave life to everything that was created, and his life*

> *brought light to everyone.* [5] *The light shines in the darkness, and the darkness can never extinguish it.* (John 1:1–5 NLT)

Before Creation, Jesus already existed.

Listen to what this is claiming. Jesus was with God before the world was created. Jesus is God. Everything that was created, including you and me, was created through Jesus. Without Jesus, we aren't here. Jesus gave life to everything. And the life that is found in Jesus brings light to everything. So let me unpack the truth we cannot afford to miss and yet that most Christians have been missing their whole lives. *Before God created you, Jesus had already agreed to die for you.* Or let me simplify that even more:

To Jesus, you have always been worth it.

He looked at humanity. He knew how we would fail. He knew what sin would do to this world. He knew that He would come to His creation and so many would reject Him. He knew our redemption would cost Him everything. He knew He would need to die so that we could live. And he didn't hesitate … not for a second.

Jesus has always been all in on you.
All He wants is for you to be all in on Him.

That's what this New Covenant is all about. It's about Jesus making a way for you to go all in on Him. And it's about you making the choice to do just that.

> *The new covenant represents the culmination of God's saving work among his people. God regenerates his people by his Spirit and renews their hearts so that they obey him. The basis for such renewal is the cross and resurrection of Jesus Christ, for by his atoning death and resurrection complete forgiveness of sins is achieved. Hence, a new and bold access to God that wasn't available in the old covenant*

> *is obtained. The covenant with Israel has passed away, and now the promise is fulfilled in the restored Israel, which consists of both Jews and Gentiles. All the promises made to Abraham and David are fulfilled in the new covenant. (Thomas R. Schreiner)*

Jesus made a way out. He made a way back. He made a way where there was no way before. He offers new life through His sacrifice. And when we enter into this covenantal relationship with Jesus, God puts his Holy Spirit IN us, giving us the strength to live in the freedom we are being offered. But here's the catch. You can't enter into this new life and this New Covenant without letting go of your old life.

> *This means that anyone who belongs to Christ has become a new person. The old life is gone; a new life has begun!* (2 Corinthians 5:17 NLT)

Everyone wants the new life Paul is talking about here. But no one is ready to let go of their old life. I feel like I've spent my entire adult life in ministry watching people almost choose Jesus. Watching them want all He is offering. Embracing all the beneficial ideas. Trying in their own strength to look like they are living a righteous life. Trying in vain to try to earn God's favor. Crushed by the weight of trying to earn the freedom that is already theirs and is freely offered, if they will just let go.

You can't choose surrender and still be in control.

To embrace one is to let go of the other. To hold fast to one is to lose the other. To be set free to be who God made you to be means letting go of control over who you become and trusting that only He can help you become who you're supposed to be. It's finding our identity in Him and not in the things of this world, or our human relationships, or our lifestyle, or our political opinions, or our sexual preferences. We are more than all of these things, and our identity can only be found in Him. So many are striving to find themselves separate from God, not realizing they can never be complete apart from Him. And what people so often fail to realize is that by not choosing to fully enter into this New Covenant with God, we are actually making a covenant with this world. There is no version of life outside of these two realities. You're giving your life to something. You're entering into a binding agreement either way.

> *It is clear that there can be but two and only two covenants possible between God and men—a covenant founded upon what man shall do for salvation, (or) a covenant founded upon what God shall do for him to save him: in other words, a Covenant of Works and a Covenant of Grace (The Divine Covenants by Arthur W. Pink)*

> *The entire ordo salutis [order of salvation], beginning with regeneration as its first stage, is bound to the mystical union with Christ. There is no gift that has not been earned by him. (J.I. Packer, An Introduction to Covenant Theology)*

At the end of the day, this comes down not to whether or not you choose a covenant but to which covenant you choose. It doesn't boil down to giving your life away or keeping it for yourself. It comes down to giving your life to Jesus or giving your life to ... well ... less. And over and over again, my heart breaks as I watch people choose less. In 2 Timothy 4, the Apostle Paul speaks of this tragic pattern in the people he was ministering to—a pattern that is still the reality today. Remember Paul's cry to all of us?

> 6 *As for me, my life has already been poured out as an offering to God. The time of my death is near.* 7 *I have fought the good fight, I have finished the race, and I have remained faithful.* (2 Timothy 4:6-7 NLT)

Paul is saying to us—"I made my choice." I had a come to Jesus moment. The scales fell off my eyes. I went all in on Jesus. I let go. I poured out my life as an offering to God. I have been faithful to my end of this covenant. But if you back up just a few verses, you hear Paul's warning, his appeal, and his desperate cry to all of us:

> [3] *For a time is coming when people will no longer listen to sound and wholesome teaching. They will follow their own desires and will look for teachers who will tell them whatever their itching ears want to hear.* [4] *They will reject the truth and chase after myths.* (2 Timothy 4:3-4 NLT)

That time is here. We are living in it. Look up. Look around. Look at the world you are living in. The world you are raising your kids in. The world where you work. The world you (far too often) seek to find meaning in. Does it seem like the way this world is choosing to do things is for your best possible good? As you hold God at arm's length, just so you can taste the "goodness" of this world, is it really good? Power corrupts. Money seduces. The world is dark. Just like in the time of the judges, everyone is doing what is right in their own eyes.

Sure, there are moments in this life, small pieces of it, that are incredible. And so we chase those moments. We live for the weekend. We chase the next big thrill. We sacrifice things that really matter, chasing the next high, the next moment. We fear death and do everything we can to fight it, avoid it, and ignore it. And when it comes (and it comes for all of us), we act surprised. We are so scared to hold this life loosely. And yet what we fail to realize is that the pleasures of this life do not last, and the moments we find are truly worth holding onto are actually just glimpses of the eternity that is being promised in Jesus. If we will just let go—of selfishness and pride. Let go of our airbrushed version of Jesus. Let go of our expectations. Let go of whatever is in your box, hidden in the shadows, making promises it can't keep. Let go of sins hidden in the dark and all the secrets. Let go of cultural Christianity that attends church on Sunday but isn't living a life of faith Monday-Saturday. Let go of the notion that Jesus can be your Savior but doesn't have to be your Lord. Let go of the lie the enemy whispers—that you can have the kingdom without the cross. Let go of half-hearted devotion, legalistic obedience, vain attempts to earn your way to heaven—let go of control ... and choose surrender.

> *"If man will acknowledge fully the lordship of the Creator by obeying his word purely for the sake of obedience, he shall experience the consummate blessing of the covenant."* (O. Palmer Robertson, *The Christ of the Covenants*)

> 6 As *for me, my life has already been poured out as an offer-*
> *ing to God. The time of my death is near.* 7 *I have fought the*
> *good fight, I have finished the race, and I have remained*
> *faithful.* 8 *And now the prize awaits me—the crown of righteousness, which the Lord, the righteous Judge, will give me on the day of his return. And the prize is not just for me but for all who eagerly look forward to his appearing.* (2 Timothy 4:6-8 NLT)

Bibliography

Bible Gateway Passage: Genesis 3 - New Living Translation. Bible Gateway. (n.d.). www.biblegateway.com/passage/?search=Genesis+3&version=NLT

Bible Gateway Passage: Romans 7 - New Living Translation. Bible Gateway, www.biblegateway.com/passage/?search=Romans+7&version=NLT. Accessed 5 Oct. 2023.

Bible Gateway Passage: Luke 14 - New Living Translation. Bible Gateway, www.biblegateway.com/passage/?search=Luke+14&version=NLT. Accessed 10 Oct. 2023.

Ferrer, Josep. "Swipe Left, Swipe Right-but Why?" Medium, UX Collective, 27 Sept. 2022, uxdesign.cc/swipe-left-swipe-right-but-why-tinder-ux-ui-simple-dating-mobile-app-swiping-design-4d2295d80407.

"Swipe Right." Urban Dictionary, www.urbandictionary.com/define.php?term=Swipe+right. Accessed 24 Oct. 2023.

"Cancel Culture." Wikipedia, Wikimedia Foundation, 19 Oct. 2023, en.wikipedia.org/wiki/Cancel_culture#:~:text=The%20expression%20%22cancel%20culture%22%20came,framing%20of%20the%20same%20concept.

"Swiping Right on Christ." Jon Sherwood, Jon Sherwood, 30 Jan. 2017, www.jonsherwood.com/post/swiping-right-on-christ.

Rashad, Chase. Seamless: What Your Spiritual Gifts Are Really For. Wesleyan Publishing House, 2023.

Bible Gateway Passage: Ephesians 5 - New Living Translation. Bible

Gateway, www.biblegateway.com/passage/?search=Ephesians+5&version=NLT. Accessed 12 Nov. 2023.

Myers, Kevin, et al. The Second Happy: Seven Practices to Make Your Marriage Better than Your Honeymoon. Nelson Books, 2022.

Transcendent - Definition, Meaning & Synonyms. Vocabulary.Com, www.vocabulary.com/dictionary/transcendent. Accessed 12 Nov. 2023.

Immanent Definition & Meaning. Merriam-Webster, Merriam-Webster, www.merriam-webster.com/dictionary/immanent. Accessed 12 Nov. 2023.

Lust. Webster's 1913, www.websters1913.com/words/Lust. Accessed 30 Nov. 2023.

Bible Gateway Passage: John 3:16 - New Living Translation. Bible Gateway, www.biblegateway.com/passage/?search=John+3%3A16&version=NLT. Accessed 7 Dec. 2023.

Bible Gateway Passage: Matthew 22 - New Living Translation. Bible Gateway, www.biblegateway.com/passage/?search=Matthew+22&version=NLT. Accessed 21 Dec. 2023.

Kelly, John. "8 Greek Words for Love That Will Make Your Heart Soar." Dictionary.Com, Dictionary.com, 2 Feb. 2022, www.dictionary.com/e/greek-words-for-love/.

Bible Gateway Passage: 1 John 4 - New Living Translation. Bible Gateway, www.biblegateway.com/passage/?search=1+John+4&version=NLT. Accessed 21 Dec. 2023.

1 Corinthians 13 NLT - - Bible Gateway, www.biblegateway.com/passage/?search=1%2BCorinthians%2B13&version=NLT. Accessed 21 Dec. 2023.

"Sacred Prostitution." Wikipedia, Wikimedia Foundation, 1 Jan. 2024, en.wikipedia.org/wiki/Sacred_prostitution.

Deuteronomy 23:17-18 NLT - - Bible Gateway, www.biblegateway.com/passage/?search=Deuteronomy%2B23%3A17-18&version=NLT. Accessed 2 Jan. 2024.

Hosea 2:14 NLT - - Bible Gateway, www.biblegateway.com/passage/?-search=Hosea%2B2%3A14&version=NLT. Accessed 2 Jan. 2024.

"Spiritual Prostitution in the Church," *Lima News*, LimaOhio.Com, 27 Aug. 2015, www.limaohio.com/uncategorized/2015/08/26/spiritual-prostitution-in-the-church/.

Bibliography

Bible Gateway Passage: John 6 - New Living Translation. Bible Gateway, www.biblegateway.com/passage/?search=John+6&version=NLT. Accessed 17 Jan. 2024.

Bible Gateway Passage: Matthew 7 - New Living Translation. Bible Gateway, www.biblegateway.com/passage/?search=Matthew+7&version=NLT. Accessed 17 Jan. 2024.

Bible Gateway Passage: Ephesians 5 - New Living Translation." Bible Gateway, www.biblegateway.com/passage/?search=Ephesians+5&version=NLT. Accessed 7 Feb. 2024.

Genesis 2 NLT - - Bible Gateway, www.biblegateway.com/passage/?-search=Genesis%2B2&version=NLT. Accessed 7 Feb. 2024.

Bible Gateway Passage: Genesis 1 - New Living Translation. Bible Gateway, www.biblegateway.com/passage/?search=Genesis+1&version=NLT. Accessed 7 Feb. 2024.

Proverbs 11:3 NIV - - Bible Gateway, www.biblegateway.com/passage/?search=proverbs%2B11%3A3&version=NIV. Accessed 9 Feb. 2024.

Chesterton, G. K. What's Wrong with the World. Dodd Mead, 1920.

Schreiner PhD, Thomas R., "10 Things You Should Know about the Biblical Covenants." Crossway, 17 July 2017, www.crossway.org/articles/10-things-you-should-know-about-the-biblical-covenants/.

"God's Covenants with Humanity." Mike Landry, mikeisthird.com/covenants/. Accessed 16 Feb. 2024.

Bible Gateway Passage: Matthew 7 - New Living Translation. Bible Gateway, www.biblegateway.com/passage/?search=Matthew+7&version=NLT. Accessed 20 Feb. 2024.

Bible Gateway Passage: John 6 - New Living Translation. Bible Gateway, www.biblegateway.com/passage/?search=John+6&version=NLT. Accessed 20 Feb. 2024.

Packer, J.I. Packer, J.I. An Introduction to Covenant Theology. CreateSpace Independent Publishing Platform, October 30, 2012.

Watkin, Christopher. Biblical Critical Theory: How the Bible's Unfolding Story Makes Sense of Modern Life and Culture. Zondervan, 2022.

Bible. Christianity.Com, www.christianity.com/wiki/bible/what-is-a-covenant-biblical-meaning-and-importance-today.htm. Accessed 23 Feb. 2024.

M., Nouwen Henri J. Bread for the Journey: Reflections for Every Day of the Year. St. Pauls, 2002.

Crisp, Oliver, and Fred Sanders. Locating Atonement: Explorations in Constructive Dogmatics. Zondervan, 2017.

Robertson, O. Palmer. The Christ of the Covenants. Presbyterian & Reformed Pub. Co., 1985.

Richter, Sandra L. The Epic of Eden: A Christian Entry into The Old Testament. IVP Academic, 2008.

Genesis 6 NLT - - Bible Gateway, www.biblegateway.com/passage/?search=Genesis%2B6&version=NLT. Accessed 1 Mar. 2024.

Woollard, Whitney. "The Five Key Covenants God Makes with Humans in the Bible." BibleProject, BibleProject, 1 Mar. 2024, bibleproject.com/articles/covenants-the-backbone-bible/.

Bible Gateway Passage: Genesis 9 - New Living Translation. Bible Gateway, www.biblegateway.com/passage/?search=Genesis+9&version=NLT. Accessed 1 Mar. 2024.

Bible Gateway Passage: Genesis 15 - New Living Translation. Bible Gateway, www.biblegateway.com/passage/?search=Genesis+15&version=NLT. Accessed 5 Mar. 2024.

Bible Gateway Passage: Genesis 17 - New Living Translation. Bible Gateway, www.biblegateway.com/passage/?search=Genesis+17&version=NLT. Accessed 5 Mar. 2024.

Bible Gateway Passage: Romans 2 - New Living Translation. Bible Gateway, www.biblegateway.com/passage/?search=Romans+2&version=NLT. Accessed 5 Mar. 2024.

Bible Gateway Passage: Judges 21 - New Living Translation. Bible Gateway, www.biblegateway.com/passage/?search=Judges+21&version=NLT. Accessed 5 Mar. 2024.

1 Samuel 8 NLT - - Bible Gateway, www.biblegateway.com/passage/?search=1%2BSamuel%2B8&version=NLT. Accessed 5 Mar. 2024.

Bible Gateway Passage: 1 Samuel 16 - New Living Translation. Bible Gateway, www.biblegateway.com/passage/?search=1+Samuel+16&version=NLT. Accessed 15 Mar. 2024.

2 Samuel 7 NLT - - Bible Gateway, www.biblegateway.com/passage/?search=2%2BSamuel%2B7&version=NLT. Accessed 15 Mar. 2024.

Bible Gateway Passage: John 1 - New Living Translation. Bible Gateway, www.biblegateway.com/passage/?search=John+1&version=NLT. Accessed 22 Mar. 2024.

2 Corinthians 5 NLT - - Bible Gateway, www.biblegateway.com/passage/?search=2%2Bcorinthians%2B5&version=NLT. Accessed 22 Mar. 2024.

About the Author

Phill Tague is the founding pastor of Ransom Church in Sioux Falls, South Dakota. He is a husband who is radically in love with his wife, Stephani, a father of three kids he could not be more proud of, and a Saul turned Paul, redeemed by a God who cared enough to stop him in his tracks, call him on his crap, and invite him into so much more.